VIEW OF
WESSEX

VIEW OF
WESSEX

Described and
photographed by
GEOFFREY N. WRIGHT

ROBERT HALE · LONDON

© *Geoffrey N. Wright 1978*
First published in Great Britain 1978

ISBN 0 7091 6372 X

Robert Hale Limited
Clerkenwell House
Clerkenwell Green
London EC1

Photoset, printed and bound
in Great Britain by
REDWOOD BURN LTD.,
Trowbridge & Esher

Frontispiece:
The Wiltshire harvest pattern on the edge of Salisbury Plain.

CONTENTS

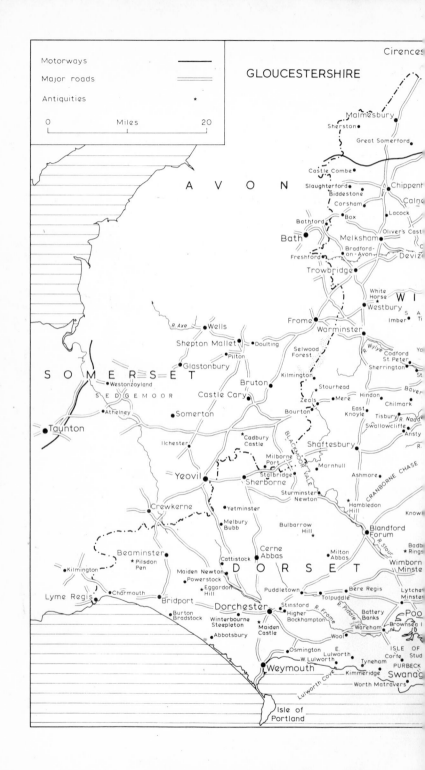

Motorways

Major roads

Antiquities

0   Miles   20

GLOUCESTERSHIRE

Cirences

A V O N

Malmesbury
Sherston
Great Somerford
Castle Combe
Slaughterford
Biddestone
Corsham
Box
Bathford
Bath
Melksham
Bradford-
on-Avon
Freshford
Trowbridge
Chippen
Caln
Lacock
Oliver's Cast
Deviz

White
Horse
Westbury
Imber
WI
S A
A
Ti

Frome
Warminster
Wells
R. Axe
Shepton Mallet
Doulting
Pilton
Glastonbury
Selwood
Forest
Kilmington
R. Wylye
Codford
St. Peter
Sherrington
St.
Ya

S O M E R S E T
Westonzoyland
Bruton
Stourhead
Zeals
Mere
Hindon
Baver
Chilmark
East
Knoyle
Tisbury
R. Nadd
Swallowcliffe
St.
Ansty
R.
SEDGEMOOR
Castle Cary
Somerton
Atheley
Bourton
Taunton
Ilchester
Cadbury
Castle
BLACKMOOR VALE
Shaftesbury
Milborne
Port
Marnhull
Ashmore
CRANBORNE CHASE
Yeovil
Stalbridge
Sherborne
Sturminster
Newton
Hambledon
Hill
Knowl
Crewkerne
Yetminster
Melbury
Bubb
Bulbarrow
Hill
Blandford
Forum
Badb
Rings
R. Stour
Beaminster
Pilsdon
Pen
Cerne
Abbas
Milton
Abbas
Wimborn
Minste
Kilmington
Cattistock
D O R S E T
Maiden Newton
Powerstock
Eggardon
Hill
Puddletown
Bere Regis
Tolpuddle
Lytche
Minste
Lyme Regis
Charmouth
Bridport
Dorchester
Stinsford
Higher
Bockhampton
R. Frome
R. Piddle
Battery
Banks
Wareham
Poo
Brownsea I
Burton
Bradstock
Winterbourne
Steepleton
Abbotsbury
Maiden
Castle
Wool
ISLE
OF
Corfe
Stud
PURBECK
Osmington
E.
Lulworth
W. Lulworth
Tyneham
Swanag
Weymouth
Kimmeridge
Worth Matravers
Lulworth Cove

Isle of
Portland

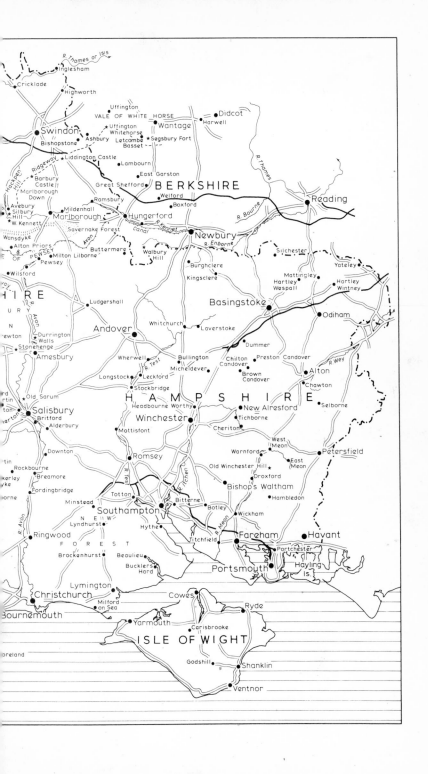

ILLUSTRATIONS

THE ANCIENT KINGDOM

ONLY WHERE it meets the sea has Wessex any definite frontier. On the north, east, and west its limits follow no tidy lines drawn either on a Boundaries Commission map, or in the charters of an ancient kingdom. Even during the centuries of its own independent existence the size of Wessex expanded or contracted according to the power of its rulers or to the strength of assaults made on it by other tribes and kingdoms. The Wessex of King Alfred certainly varied in this way; Thomas Hardy's Wessex has never strictly been defined. Yet when we refer to the area today we have a good idea of what we mean, and recognize that the name Wessex correctly implies a degree of unity, even though this may be less than it used to be.

The Anglo-Saxons who colonized so much of southern England were not only seafarers and fighters but great farmers, the best this island had ever known. They loved the land, the tending of its soil and the care of its livestock. Working together they cleared forests

The view south-west from the ramparts of the Iron Age hill-fort on Cley Hill near Warminster, Wiltshire.

and woodlands, settled in small communities, and gradually created the countryside, writing on it the pattern of village and farmstead, pasture and ploughland. Today, more than a thousand years later, most of Wessex is still an agricultural area. This is one of the facets of its unity, emphasized by the fact that the largest towns – Southampton, Portsmouth, Bournemouth, Swindon, together with the peripheral ones of Bath and Reading – have very little in common with the rest of Wessex. Unlike, say, Norwich with East Anglia, Leeds with West Yorkshire, or Bristol with the West of England, individual identities of Wessex towns have been almost swamped by their recent artificial growth.

It is in the smaller towns, whose roots lie in the countryside, who serve its needs and receive some of its sustenance, where lies so much of another facet of the character of Wessex.

The country towns of Dorset, Wiltshire, and Hampshire are as fine as any in England, and these three counties form the main core of Wessex. For the purposes of this book, part of East Somerset must be included, for Alfred himself has strong links with the Somerset fenlands, while Arthur's connections with Cadbury and Glastonbury cannot be ignored. Part of the new county of Avon comes into the survey, for it must be remembered that the first king of all England was crowned at Bath. St Aldhelm was one of the great missionaries and scholars of Saxon Wessex, and his influence originated from Malmesbury, very near the Gloucestershire border; and returning to Alfred, his early years at Wantage justify part of Berkshire as far north as the Thames being regarded as fair Wessex territory. On the east, the present Hampshire border with Sussex is a natural limit to Wessex wanderings, and there is no really good reason for excluding the Isle of Wight. There, then, is the Wessex of this survey, about 4,000 square miles of English countryside.

To start with the rocks beneath. Chalk is one of the chief unifying features of the Wessex landscape, for at its geographical centre is the great plateau of Salisbury Plain. Ranges of chalk radiate from there in most directions, northwards to the Marlborough Downs which in turn throw out a long finger from Wiltshire into Berkshire, as the White Horse Hill, their scarp-face overlooking the

Waves of Wessex chalk on the northern edge of the escarpment near Uffington, Berkshire.

clayey Vale of White Horse watered by the Thames. Along these chalk uplands ran one of the great trackways of prehistoric England, the Ridgeway.

South-west from Salisbury Plain the chalk leads from Wiltshire

The curving ridge of the chalk which forms the northern rampart of the Isle of Purbeck: looking east to Corfe, with storm-clouds over Studland, Dorset. The chalk separates the heath to the north from the Isle of Purbeck to the south.

into Dorset, reaching the coast between Bridport and Weymouth. On its way, it throws up a series of important hills, many of which reach 800 feet, with Bulbarrow and Pilsdon Pen over 900 feet. From near Beaminster the South Dorset Downs run south-eastwards to Purbeck where they create a smoothly rounded rim of chalk which separates the 'Isle of Purbeck' from sandy heath-lands to the north.

Salisbury Plain extends eastwards into Hampshire, where it separates into the North and South Downs, eventually reaching the sea at Dover and Beachy Head respectively. Thus it is almost possible to travel the length and breadth of Wessex on the chalk. Near where some of the chalklands end, limestone country takes over, especially to the west and north, where the Jurassic limestone belt runs from west Dorset through eastern Somerset and west Wiltshire, to the Cotswolds and beyond. Never reaching the same height as the chalk, it nevertheless introduces scenic variety, and more importantly, fine building stones, especially valuable since chalk itself is not a particularly good material for house con-struction.

A third geological contrast arises from the acid soils, sandy heaths, and often boggy countryside of the New Forest and south-east Dorset. Mingled with these major features are the dreamy, lush landscapes of the clay vales, the belts of greensand country which often form benches round the edge of the chalk, and the intensive horticultural area of the Hampshire basin and parts of the Isle of Wight.

Although so large an area of Wessex is formed of the fossilized remains of marine creatures of millions of years ago, nowhere in the region now quite reaches 1,000 feet above sea level. The high-est point in Wessex, indeed on any of the English chalklands, is Walbury Hill, 975 feet, near the Berkshire–Wiltshire border. Chalk is porous, so most of the rain which falls upon it sinks into the ground, eventually to meet impervious strata, often very far down beneath the surface. Above this layer water slowly accumu-lates in pores and crevices of rock until saturation occurs. Above this saturated zone is a damper zone where rain water is gradually percolating, and between these two zones is a definite level of demarcation called the water-table, which varies according to the amount of rain which has fallen. After a prolonged wet spell this rises; following a dry season it falls.

This fluctuating water-table affects the streams and rivers of the chalk which flow in only a few of the many valleys. Most valleys in the chalklands are dry, and constitute one of its significant scenic features. Some chalk-streams flow only during and after very wet seasons, such water-courses being known as 'bournes', giving rise to the many 'Bourne' place-names in the three main counties. Usually the water-table is nearer to the surface in a valley than on the uplands, making it easier to obtain water from wells in the valley bottoms, encouraging the formation of settlements there, while leaving the higher chalk country largely unpopulated. But as these uplands became the great grazing lands for flocks of sheep, and more recently herds of cattle, their lack of surface water made it necessary to create the many dew-ponds which still survive.

Wessex boasts the two classic chalk streams beloved by trout-fishermen, the Test and the Itchen. But there are others, lesser known yet still characteristic — Wylye and Frome, Stour and Kennet, Bourne and Avon, and the Meon which Izaak Walton fished — whose valleys provide soft, pastoral scenery of the southern and central parts of Wessex.

However, it is not in the valleys that the human associations with Wessex have their distant origins, but on the chalk itself. There, above the swamps and dense forests of the vales, a shallow soil could be tilled by crude implements, sheep would graze a fine turf, and flints existed which could be used as simple tools and weapons. Flint is a hard siliceous rock, insoluble, immensely durable, which exists as nodules or in beds within the chalk, so that the chalk areas attracted early settlers in our island.

Salisbury Plain became their metropolis. As we have already seen, chalk ridges radiate from the Plain, and these became the natural causeways along which nomadic peoples could move. Woodlands on the thin dry soils of the chalk were much easier to clear than those of the marshy vales, so that as a result central Wiltshire now shows more evidence of prehistoric occupations over a long period of time than anywhere else in England. Hill-top

The Kennet and Avon Canal at Horton, near Devizes, Wiltshire.

Overleaf: *A snow-mantle on Stonehenge.*

camps, tumuli, trackways, and monuments are all signposts to its ancient importance.

The first farmers in Wessex were probably Neolithic immigrants from Europe who had reached us in the fourth millennium B.C. Very little indeed is known about them, but later settlers have certainly been traced to Wiltshire. Windmill Hill, $1\frac{1}{2}$ miles northwest of Avebury, is a low rounded hill crowned by three concentric rings of causewayed ditches, the whole area covering 21 acres. The site was systematically excavated in the 1920s, and is now known to be the earliest Neolithic settlement in Britain. Avebury Museum houses many of the finds from Windmill Hill, including pottery dated to about 2500 B.C., and the excavations showed that the Windmill Hill people kept sheep, pigs, small long-horned

*West Kennet Long Barrow, near Avebury, Wiltshire — showing the
portal stone with the entrance to the barrow in shade (left).*

cattle, and dogs, and that they grew wheat, barley, and flax.

Almost a thousand years separate Windmill Hill from the more famous prehistoric monument at Avebury – about the same length of time by which we are removed from the Norman Conquest. We know of the continuity of life during these nine centuries; we know very little of what happened during that millennium between the Neolithic and Bronze Ages. The chalklands were never devoid of life, so we can only assume that some form of farming was carried on for scores of generations. We do know that people buried their dead in long barrows, low mounds near the surface of the chalk, now grass-grown. Broader and higher at the end where burials occurred, some have stone chambers, like that so splendidly excavated at West Kennet, opposite Silbury Hill, and some have stone floors. Many have been used for successive burials; others, like the huge one near Winterborne Stoke, contain only one burial.

Thus, on the chalky uplands of Wiltshire man was beginning to impose his ideas on the environment where he lived. Simple tilling of fields, nibbling away by livestock of downland bushes and scrub, the building of simple beehive-shaped huts, digging of flints, and burial of the dead. A pattern of life and death was being evolved, and the most basic foundations of a nation were being laid.

Later invaders, coming from Eastern Europe by the Low Countries, and across the narrow Channel, moved into southern England. These Beaker Folk, so named from the drinking vessels that were buried with them, brought new skills, new ways of life. Nomadic pastoralists, capable of waging war with bows and arrows, later with axes and bronze implements, they were also concerned with the great mysteries of life and death. To them, the sun was the only source of all life, and to its worship they built in Britain a number of henge monuments, of which the greatest were Stonehenge and Avebury.

A henge is a circle, usually of stone but sometimes of wood, within an earthen bank, having at least one entrance. Those with a single entrance are older than those with more. Just as, say a cathedral may contain building styles covering perhaps three or four

Continuity of use of an ancient sacred site: at Knowlton, Dorset, a fourteenth-century church (now ruined) lies inside a prehistoric circle.

hundred years, from Norman to Perpendicular, so do these great prehistoric shrines reveal a similar period of growth and development. Stonehenge represents as much as five centuries of worship by changing cultures, from about 1900–1400 B.C. Avebury spans half of this, say 1700–1500 B.C.

Situated within the fork where the main A303 divides, west of Amesbury, Stonehenge seems small against the far horizons of the Plain. But once you leave the car in a large car park, which always seems full, and invariably has an ice-cream van, and walk through the tunnel beneath the road, the whole perspective changes. The huge stones look down to the wandering, wondering humans. Hands touch the hard sarsens hauled across the Plain, and the smaller blue Pembrokeshire stones of the inner groups; heads gaze upwards, or are downcast into the cold print of guidebooks.

Nothing, however, can detract from the powerful awe and mystery, accentuated when the low angle of sunlight lengthens shadows of the stones so that they touch the outer ditch. There are few passages in literature which so finely evoke the atmosphere of Stonehenge as Hardy's description of the arrival of Tess and Angel, in the dark, at the great monument on Wiltshire's chalk.

Avebury's circle of stones was much larger, and now encloses part of the village. About thirty stones remain to give a good impression of the immense physical task of moving and erecting them. Their source was quite local, within two or three miles dry valleys in the Marlborough Downs still have hundreds of sarsen stones. 'Sarsen' is the lazy Wiltshire corruption of 'saracen', meaning a foreigner. These boulders of hard, siliceous sandstone are foreign to the native soft white chalk.

Avebury, Wiltshire: part of the south-west sector of the stone circle, with evening shadows lying long on the grass.

Impressive as the Avebury Circle is, and it takes you about a quarter of an hour to walk round its outer embankment, it lacks the sombre solitude of Stonehenge. Trees and cottages are friendly neighbours to the male and female stones, and the nearby church nods its own benediction to the ancient temple. Avebury's bisexual element is also apparent in the stones of its Avenue to the south-west. Although many are missing, sufficient remain to amplify Avebury's importance as one of the major prehistoric complexes in Europe.

Silbury Hill is obviously part of it, and remains the biggest enigma of all. Two centuries of intermittent excavations have yielded very little of interest except to indicate that the 130-foot high man-made mound was built in four continuous stages, probably around 2100 B.C., and that a million cubic yards of chalk had to be excavated in its construction. The steep climb up its grassy sides gives the reward of a fine view down the valley of the infant Kennet, and a visual proof that the A4, following the line of the old Roman road, certainly detours round the base of Silbury Hill.

Speeding traffic on this road misses the tiny henge monument known as the Sanctuary on Overton Hill, where the Ridgeway comes down from the chalk to cross the Kennet. Durrington Walls, near Amesbury, is another henge, a third of a mile across, and retaining its outer banks and ditch, while at Knowlton, near Cranborne, on the Dorset chalk, one of the embanked circles has the medieval church, now ruined, inside it. Maumbury Rings is between Dorchester's two railway stations, and was a Neolithic henge monument taken over by the Romans and used as a theatre, while Eggardon Hill, commanding one of the most widespread views in Wessex, subsequently became an Iron Age hillfort.

Woodhenge, immediately to the south-west of Durrington Walls, may originally have been a large circular building, partly roofed, and having an open central courtyard. The whole lay within a bank and ditch nearly 60 yards in diameter, and the pottery finds from the site, now in Devizes Museum, point to its period and occupation extending from 2000 to 1600 B.C.

Farming became quite settled as the Bronze Age progressed.

Silbury Hill, Wiltshire — still an enigma after 3,500 years.

Improved techniques of working metal resulted in better tools and implements being made. Travelling smiths and traders began to visit Britain, and gradually new invaders came here to settle peacefully, to work the land and to trade. By the end of the sixth century B.C. groups of iron-using people from France and the Alps reached our shores, bringing their new materials with them. Landing along our eastern and southern coasts they soon spread inland to live in farms and small communities. They grew corn and hay, kept cattle and sheep in bigger numbers than earlier folk had done, but fewer pigs. This suggests that there was more open pasture, less thick woodland.

All over their settlement area they built hillforts, in the form of

Wayland Smith's Cave, near Uffington, Berkshire: a prehistoric long-barrow situated close to the Ridgeway.

enclosures within ditches and embankments, where whole communities could seek refuge against other groups of Iron Age settlers from different parts of the Continent, and having slightly different cultures. Many of these were from north-west France and Brittany, and landed in the western parts of Britain. From the second century B.C. a third group of settlers crossed the sea to us, the Belgae from north-east France and Belgium, bringing new ideas, new cultures, and newer farming methods involving a much heavier plough which enabled them to turn the soil, making it possible for valleys to be cultivated and occupied. The successive waves of Iron Age immigrants overlapped one another, as did their cultures, and together that made a strong impact on the Wessex landscape, particularly in Dorset and Wiltshire.

For more than a thousand years southern Britain in general, and the Wessex chalklands in particular, had been the home of Bronze Age people. They had worshipped the sun in their great circular temples, their flocks and herds had nibbled the short turf, had provided them with food and clothing. Their metal-smiths, first in bronze and later in copper, had fashioned weapons, tools, and implements. Their traders travelled the green tracks which followed the watersheds radially from Salisbury Plain, and it is along these upland trade routes that most of the hillforts of the later Iron Age dwellers are situated.

Spreading outwards from Salisbury Plain the old trackways led along the upland ridges to the prehistoric ports and harbours of the Channel and North Sea coasts, to the estuaries of Thames and Severn, to the limestone hills of Cotswold, and beyond to the Midlands. They only left the hills where it was necessary to cross river valleys. Names were given to these highways by our Anglo-Saxon ancestors: Ridgeway, Harroway (hard way), Herepath (through road, or war road). Chalk being porous, the old routes across the uplands rarely became waterlogged; ridges and hollows made by feet of animals and humans would be smoothed out by frost. Long periods of usefulness may have been followed by equally long silences, but throughout the passing centuries the ancient ways survived.

Thus, by following such trackways today we can reach back

through the misty centuries, time-travellers as it were, stopping off at any period we like. A few years ago the Countryside Commission designated the most famous of these, the great Ridgeway, as a long-distance footpath running for 85 miles from Overton Hill near Avebury to Ivinghoe Beacon in the Chilterns. For nearly half of this distance, along the crest of the North Wessex Downs, as far as the Thames at Goring, it is a bridle-path and rough-riders' route for cyclists too. Since it crosses a number of main roads motorists have plenty of access points from which they, too, can explore windy solitudes of the chalk escarpment, and feel beneath the feet over thirty centuries of human and animal movements.

I prefer to walk it westwards, with the wind in my face, and Avebury as my goal. Once the Thames is left behind there are no villages along the way, and the broad track gradually gains height to Lowbury Hill and Blewbury Down. Industrial Didcot, atomic plant Harwell, and eventually more ancient Wantage lie only a few miles away from the foot of the downs. Across the busy A34, then the B4494 and A338, the Ridgeway touches the southern earthworks of Segsbury hillfort above the great green basin where Letcombe Bassett lazes its years away. Another main road, B4001, at the top of Hackpen Hill, brings racehorses from the many stables around here and at Lambourn, for their training gallops on the crisp springy turf.

Then a northward arc by White Horse Hill brings the Ridgeway within easy reach of the oldest of the chalk down figures, so prominent in the view of the northern edge of the downs from the lush pastures of the Vale of White Horse. Just as the ancient trackways on the Wessex chalklands tend to link the thirty or more Iron Age hillforts, so can they be used to visit most of the 'white horses' and other hill figures that decorate some of the steeper slopes. Uffington's White Horse, 365 feet from ear to tail, and almost bird-headed, probably dates from late Iron Age times, and can reasonably be explained as being the tribal emblem of the Dobunni or Atribates who occupied the adjacent hillfort.

Westwards from Uffington the Ridgeway soon passes Wayland's Smithy, a chambered long barrow where erosion has revealed many stones used in its construction, and excavations

The Ridgeway above Avebury, Wiltshire, Sarsen stones can be seen beside the ancient track.

revealed fourteen burials there, probably from between 3500 B.C. and 3000 B.C. The legend of Wayland the Smith seems to have originated in Saxon times, but has been referred to since then by a number of writers, including Scott in *Kenilworth* and Thomas Hughes in *Tom Brown's Schooldays*. Hughes, of course, spent his boyhood in Uffington. Country folk believed that if a traveller required his horse to be shod, he should tie it to an upright sarsen, place a coin (probably a groat) on the flat stone nearby, and leave. On returning ten minutes later he would find his horse newly shod, the money gone, and no sign of the famous smith.

The direct line of the Ridgeway runs south-westwards from Wayland's Smithy, past another prominent hillfort, Liddington Castle, to Barbury Castle. But between these two Iron Age settlements the ancient track keeps to lower ground nearer the foot of the escarpment, and for some distance has metalled roads imposed upon it. The official long-distance bridleway has been given a big southwards diversion to the Ogbournes, near Marlborough, then following the crest of Smeathe's Ridge to Barbury, where it rejoins the old way. Wiltshire County Council have created a Country Park at Barbury, and now the Iron Age fort, with its magnificent panoramic views, is a lively place at summer weekends, and the M4 to the north carries its modern metallic burdens to east and west.

On Hackpen Hill, between Barbury and Avebury Down, the Ridgeway reaches its highest point, over 900 feet. Past beech clumps, the broad green track then swings gently downwards, with sarsen stones lying amid the grass and gorse, until it reaches the Herepath, above Avebury, with the Fyfield Down Nature Reserve immediately to the east. Although the long-distance footpath ends near here, the old way continues, no longer waymarked, south and west, crossing the more recent Wansdyke, reaching the crest of the Marlborough Downs near Milk Hill, 964 feet, before crossing Pewsey Vale by a sketchy route, and reaches Salisbury Plain by Broadbury Banks above Wilsford. On the forbidden territories of War Department land, past Imber to the downland edge at Battlebury Hill, the Ridgeway continues its southerly course towards the head of the Wylye valley, by East Knoyle.

When the enclosure movements of the eighteenth and nineteenth centuries made new patterns on the landscape, many of the green roads of the Wessex hills had their boundaries defined by low banks and hedges to prevent travellers encroaching on the newly enclosed fields. Sometimes deviations from the original routes were made to take the new line round, instead of through, an estate, an early form of bypass in fact. Occasionally, a new turnpike road followed the ancient track, but more often it took a lower-level course, bringing it through towns and villages. But since so much of Wessex is upland country, and the old ways were very direct, some of the 'flying coaches' stuck to them. You can find a number of eighteenth-century milestones along the Harroway and the Ox Drive, both in south Wiltshire. Shepherds and drovers liked to use the chalkways since their surface was good for unshod beasts, which could also find grazing along them, and the drovers could avoid paying turnpike fees.

You could enjoy an unusual Iron Age holiday visiting the fifty or so hillforts throughout Wessex. From Old Winchester Hill, near the Meon Valley in Hampshire, westwards through Wiltshire, to the greatest of them all, Maiden Castle, near Dorchester, would be a fascinating tour demanding that at every hill-top fort the motor car must be abandoned in favour of walking. I have a shrewd idea that the sum total of all the views obtained would probably embrace the whole of Wessex, except perhaps for some parts of the coast, and the north-west sector around the eastern edge of the Mendips.

There would be unusual variety, too. A number of hill-top sites have become country parks, such as Barbury, on the Ridgeway above Swindon; White Horse Hill, Uffington, and White Horse Hill, Westbury; Oliver's Castle, on the edge of Roundway Down, Devizes. These all echo, on fine summer weekends, to the sounds of twentieth-century man enjoying his recreation. At some of them you can expect to see hundreds of cars parked, their occupants, full of the pioneering spirit of exploration, even venturing as much as a quarter of a mile from them, silently watched by the sad and wondering eyes of the ghosts of two and a half thousand years ago. At Yarnbury Castle, close to the A303 on Salisbury

The Harroway on Mere Down, Wiltshire. A 1750 milestone shows that it served as a turnpike road two centuries ago.

Overleaf: The Dorset landscape – the motorist's view from the A35 on Askerwell Down, west of Dorchester.

Swirling mist adds mystery and melancholy to the view over historic Maiden Castle, Dorset.

Plain, a big sheep fair was held annually right up to the end of last century. Old Winchester Hill forms part of a large and important national nature reserve; Badbury Rings, easily accessible from the main road between Wimborne and Blandford, triple-ringed and tree-covered, is inevitably a popular place, not least as part of a point-to-point course used by a number of hunts between March and May.

Unhappily many of Dorset's old hillforts have succumbed to the plough. During the 1950s and 1960s, with the aid of government grants of up to £12 an acre for ploughing, green downland sheep-walks have been turned into more profitable arable land. The land still has a beauty which changes with the seasons, but insensitivity to landscape has lost us some priceless heritage. The great cause-

Pilsdon Pen, Dorset, looking east across Marshwood Vale. This is one of many Iron Age hillforts in Wessex.

wayed camp on Hambledon Hill has been irreparably damaged, while Eggardon and Rawlsbury have lost their ramparts. Barbed wire is an unlovely substitute for a great earthen bank; at Maiden Castle enormous wire fences surround the greatest earthwork in Britain, to keep out modern vandals, a sad but effective way to preserve a few green historic hill-top acres.

Old Sarum was a splendid site for an Iron Age hillfort. The Romans may have chosen it for their Sorviodunum, and in the seventh century it became a small Anglo-Saxon hill-top town. Its site appealed to the Normans who added a motte to the existing ramparts, established a castle, and built a cathedral, soon after the Conquest. One hundred and fifty years later, after continual friction between king and bishops, a new cathedral and a new city were planned by the Avon meadows two miles south. Seventeen centuries of occupation of Old Sarum came to an end, and now, within the grassy enclosure, the ground-plan of the Norman cathedral and fragments of castle walls survive, strangely insignificant beside the huge earthen banks.

Many miles to the west, among the green hills of Somerset, Cadbury Castle shows its own continuity. Neolithic man certainly camped there about 3500 B.C., and the site was intermittently used until late Bronze Age times, when it became permanently settled. Later Iron Age occupants built its first fortifications, involving hundreds of wooden posts, and thousands of feet of planking for shoring up the embankments round a 1,200-yard perimeter defence. Later, after being ruined for a while, stone ramparts were built, gradually being added to, up to the Roman occupation, by when Cadbury was a hill-top town inhabited by the nation of Durotriges, whose capital was at Maiden Castle. There, excavations revealed that the Romans massacred the inhabitants soon after A.D. 43. Yet at Cadbury, a similar battle against the defenders did not take place for another thirty years. Survivors dispersed to surrounding villages, and the Iron Age hillfort remained deserted for the next four centuries. This is probably a similar story as to what happened to most of the hillforts following the Roman occupation. Their tribal inhabitants slaughtered, or dispersed, they fell into a long silence, which in most cases has continued down to the present day.

There is little doubt that Iron Age people inhabited much of lowland Wessex, too. Their tribal centres and towns were on the hills, and these sites survive only because they were not inhabited or used much by later settlers. But subsequent settlement and cultivation have obscured the lowland sites so that it is only by occasional finds that evidence points to the continuous use of better lands. Thus, by the time of the Roman occupation, Wessex was reasonably well peopled, perhaps more so in Dorset than the other counties. Once the initial impact of the Roman conquest was over, three centuries of relative peace followed, with a consequent steady growth in population. More land was farmed, more settlements established, and new archaeological evidence suggests that

The view south from the ramparts of Cadbury Castle, Somerset, showing one of the high banks and ditches used in defence.

many villages and hamlets of today, previously thought to have been first settled in Saxon days, are now proving to have been occupied at least in late Roman times. As Dr W. G. Hoskins has emphasized, much of England is much older than we think.

No matter who were the overlords, land had still to be culti-vated and livestock tended. When the Romans came to Britain there was no instant transition to peace and civil order. The new rulers adapted the foundation of small states into which the country was divided, and superimposed on them their own pattern of administration based on cantons. Parts of Hampshire, Wiltshire and north Somerset formed the Belgae canton, based on Winches-ter, parts of south and east Somerset, together with east Devon and Dorset, was the Kingdom of the Durotriges, centred on Dorches-ter and Ilchester. The rest of Hampshire and Wiltshire, together with Berkshire, had its cantonal capital at Silchester. Just beyond the northern edge of Wessex, Cirencester was one of the most im-portant of all Roman towns, while on the coast, the Roman fort of Portchester was the westernmost of a chain of nine coastal defences against Saxon pirates.

Linking these Roman centres was a fine road system, followed by many of today's major highways. Look at the 1-inch or 1:50,000 Ordnance Survey maps for the relevant areas and you will see how modern roads radiating from Winchester and Dor-chester in particular adopt the original Roman alignment. The A33 north from Winchester was the way to Silchester, southwards it led to Bitterne, on a loop of the Itchen, formerly a Roman walled town. The Roman road to Salisbury is still followed in sections by metalled, if minor, modern roads. Arrowing its way north-west from Winchester, the B3420 aligns itself for a few miles exactly on the road to Mildenhall, near Marlborough, and Corinium (Ciren-cester), a wonderfully direct route as far as hilly country near Savernake, when it deviates to avoid some steep gradients.

The A35 eastwards from Dorchester first takes the line of the Roman road to Badbury Rings and Old Sarum, and westwards

Surviving vestiges of the Foss Way, seen from Beacon Hill, Shepton Mallet, Somerset.

Overleaf: *The view over Selwood Forest from Long Knoll, near Maiden Bradley, Wiltshire, showing Little Knoll (left) and the edge of the down beyond the upper reaches of the River Wylye.*

48

towards Exeter. When we drive south by the A354 to Weymouth, we are in the tracks of the Romans who went to Radipole, while northwards, the A37 points us on the Roman road to Bath, its northern section apparently lost beneath the gentle fields of west Wiltshire and east Somerset, a part of which has been painstakingly identified by Brian Berry in his rewarding little book *Discovering a Lost Roman Road*. We must not forget the Foss Way surging north-east from Axemouth to Ilchester and Bath, to Cirencester, Leicester and Lincoln, nor must we fail to recognize the recreational importance of the hot springs of Aquae Sulis for these are not just a relatively recent innovation in Wessex tourism. Within the walled town of Bath, where hot healing waters bubbled to the surface, the Romans created a complex of baths, and a temple to Sul Minerva. Aquae Sulis became an administrative centre, and a health resort for leading Roman citizens and soldiers.

At Dorchester, a wall was built to enclose the Roman town; the old earthworks of Maumbury Rings became an amphitheatre, and the town obtained its water supply by means of an aqueduct from many miles away. Near the present County Hall can be seen part of a Roman villa, including its fine tessellated pavement, and in Dorchester Museum many exhibits underline the town's former Roman importance.

Winchester's Roman remains are few, and in the far north of Hampshire, Silchester — once you can manage to find your way to it by a mazy, crazy network of lanes — is largely farmland and fields. However, to the south of the village church there is a magnificent length of wall of the original Roman town, chalk rubble and flint. The south gate is well revealed, helping to compensate for the fact that down its eastern length the wall, though still impressive, is overgrown and decaying, visible only occasionally beyond a high hedge bordering the quiet road which runs parallel to it. Bold, unhappy notices warn would-be trespassers that this is private property, a pathetic epitaph to what could be another two or three hundred yards of Roman wall. No wonder the drooping trees look sad.

The might of Imperial Rome is much more strongly felt at Portchester. On a promontory surrounded on three sides by the sea a

Portchester Castle, Hampshire, showing Roman masonry in the outer wall of the huge fort.

great Roman fort was built, mostly towards the end of the third century, and transformed in the twelfth century into a formidable castle. The whole of the Roman defensive wall survives, 10 feet thick, 20 feet high, and still having fourteen of the original twenty bastions. When Henry I adapted the Roman fort to his own needs, most of the 9-acre area within the walls became the outer bailey, separated by a moat from the newer walled-off inner bailey, with its massive Norman keep. At the opposite south-eastern corner of the Roman fort an Augustinian Priory was founded in 1133, taking over an existing Norman church which served both as a parish church and chapel for the castle.

At Bath, the Roman walled town lasted for nearly 400 years, and then was buried beneath subsequent settlements, until the eighteenth century, yet not until 1871 was its real significance realized. Excavations then revealed the Great Bath, 80 feet by 40 feet, and 6 feet deep, fed by hot water which even today continues to flow through some of the original lead conduit. Adjoining the Great Bath is the Circular Bath, 19 feet across and 5 feet deep, and nearby are cold plunge baths. Subsequent excavations have brought to light steam baths, small cold baths, hypocausts, and mosaic pavements, altogether comprising the most comprehensive nonmilitary Roman remains in Britain, yet still only a part of the whole complex of which so much still lies beneath the streets and pavements of modern Bath lying south and east of the existing Roman baths.

Taking Wessex as a whole, archaeological evidence has revealed several hundred sites, outside the important Roman towns, which were occupied in Roman times. Centuries of peace which their rule brought to a group of warring tribes inevitably led to a population increase, and the extending of frontiers of farming, down from the chalk uplands into the river valleys. It would appear that the new lowland farms and estates were more sophisticated than those which continued to occupy the higher sites. By the end of Roman times, some farmers began to move away from the hills of Dorset and Hampshire. Valleys were better drained, woods slowly cleared, and implements improved, so that marginal farming techniques on their chalk soils were slowly abandoned with the result that a 'medieval' pattern of settlement was beginning to show itself in some areas of Wessex very much earlier than was previously thought.

Over a hundred Roman villas have been identified, and some excavated, in Wessex, more than half of them in Hampshire. Most of them have occupied well-drained sites, usually within fifteen miles of one of the Roman towns that served as market centres to a largely agricultural population. None of the villa sites had been restored or is open to show anything of its past, but a number of them may have formed the very early core of much later medieval manors and estates, thus underlining the continuity of life in a suitable environment.

After the Roman armies were withdrawn early in the fifth century, almost 200 years were to elapse before the Saxon invasions seriously affected much of Wessex. For six or seven generations Roman-British life continued with very little break, although Saxons had conquered and settled widely through Hampshire and Wiltshire. Historians have difficulties in fixing key dates, but one is certain. The Anglo-Saxon Chronicle gives 577 as the year when, as a result of a battle at Dyrham, north of Bath, the Saxons gained control of that area. Until 658, when the Saxon King Kenwalh invaded Somerset, the Forest of Selwood, on the Wiltshire–Somerset border south of Bath, probably acted as a frontier zone between Wessex and the land of the West Britons. It may well have been debatable territory a lot earlier during the time of the half-legendary Arthur, with Cadbury Castle away to the south guarding the eastern approach to Somerset.

Leslie Alcock's excavations at Cadbury, 1966–70, proved that the Iron Age hillfort was reoccupied in the late fifth or early sixth centuries, with massive wooden fortifications on the ramparts of an 18-acre site. Foundations of a large hall were discovered, appropriate to a Dark Age chieftain; the whole site was large enough to accommodate a 1,000-strong army which such a leader could command. So it would seem that in this western frontier zone between Wessex and the squabbling Celtic kingdoms, there was a great military leader who gathered about him a large band of followers, and who moved widely about Britain fighting the Saxon invaders.

The last of his twelve great victories was at Mount Badon, on the north Wiltshire Downs, probably in the year 518.

Although the Saxon armies had occupied Hampshire and Wiltshire, Dorset seems to have held out against them for a considerable time, almost certainly as a result of the protection given to the area by the Bokerley Dyke. This great linear earthwork in the north-east of the county was built originally in late Roman times to block any invasion along the Dorchester–Salisbury Roman road or the downland adjoining it. It runs for six miles from the woods of Cranborne Chase to the edge of the heathlands, and is particularly easy to identify on the downs between Pentridge and Martin, where it is taken by the line of the county boundary. The Saxons from Wessex did not succeed in breaching the defences of Bokerley Dyke until almost the end of the sixth century, but it was almost another 100 years before complete Saxon domination of Dorset was eventually achieved.

The village pond at Ashmore, 700 feet up in north Dorset, a settlement probably occupied since Roman times.

CHAPTER 2

KINGS AND BISHOPS

THE LAST PART of Wessex to yield to the Saxons was probably the heathland country of south-east Dorset. Battery Banks is a ridge-top earthwork between the Rivers Frome and Piddle which may have been a last defensive structure of the Roman-British. In Wareham the Saxon church of Lady St Mary contains a number of Christian memorial inscriptions dating from the seventh to the ninth centuries, some of which are Celtic in form and lettering, evidence that there was a British population there surviving after the Saxon conquest. In addition, the church itself, of seventh-century origin, suggests that missionaries of the faith were following hard upon the heels of the conquerors.

In those distant days when not only Wessex but all England became a Christian country, the early Benedictine monasteries were lighthouses of learning and culture in a confused world. With their universal Latin language they maintained a flow of ideas between one country and another, and from one generation to the next. It is from the written records of a much later historian, William of Malmesbury, that we know so much about the life of Aldhelm, a

The Saxon church of St Martin, Wareham, Dorset.

Remains of Malmesbury's abbey, built on the site of a Saxon monastery associated with St Aldhelm.

Opposite: *Bradford-on-Avon, Wiltshire – the Saxon church founded by St Aldhelm about AD 700, though most of the masonry is about AD 1000.*

kinsman of Ine, King of Wessex (688–725), and by visiting some of the places associated with Aldhelm we can see another aspect of Wessex.

We should go first to Malmesbury in the north of Wiltshire, where Aldhelm was born in 639 and educated. He subsequently went to Canterbury where he gained a reputation as a scholar, and where he started to write letters, verses, and learned discourses. He was a talented musician, minstrel and preacher, a devout man, who in 675 was ordained priest, and returned to Malmesbury as the new monastery's first abbot. He introduced Benedictine rule, increased the monastic community, and from Malmesbury established two

new religious centres, at Frome and Bradford-on-Avon; and it is in the delightful small stone-built town by the River Avon, twenty miles south of Malmesbury, that Aldhelm founded an ecclesiola. Near to the river, Aldhelm's Saxon church retains the original plan and lower stages of the early seventh century, and the narrow openings between nave and chancel, and nave and porticus, are of Aldhelm's time. To walk through them is to move through nearly thirteen centuries, although the building was used for secular purposes for several hundred years.

Aldhelm rebuilt Malmesbury Abbey, but subsequent fires destroyed all of his work there, and the present structure represents the splendid fragments of the great Norman reconstruction. During his thirty years at Malmesbury, Aldhelm travelled widely. One visit took him to Rome, and it was while waiting at Wareham for a favourable wind that Aldhelm built a church there.

In 705 Aldhelm was consecrated first bishop of the new Diocese

St Aldhelm's chapel (late twelfth century) on The Headland, Dorset.

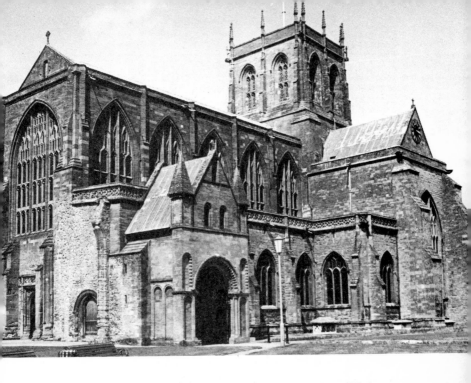

Sherborne Abbey, Dorset, the site of the first bishopric held by St Aldhelm.

of Sherborne, where, although he was by now an old man, he worked with his usual zest. He built the first cathedral, of which the present Abbey Church was a Norman replacement, as well as a house for clergy, probably on the site of the present vicarage. While he was visiting the western part of his diocese, in 709, Aldhelm died at Doulting, a hill-top village to the east of Shepton Mallet, in Somerset. When his body was taken back to Malmesbury for burial, crosses were erected at nightly halting-places, but neither the sites nor fragments of these now survive.

Travelling through Wessex today emphasizes what a strongly rural area it is, with hundreds of villages that were mainly established during Anglo-Saxon times, representing a gradual in-filling of the countryside. The population of England probably doubled from the end of Roman times to the Norman Conquest, when it reached about $1\frac{1}{4}$ million. Most of the Saxon settlements in Wessex were in the valleys, but a number of hill-top villages were almost certainly inhabited continuously since Roman days. Ashmore, the highest village in Dorset, on the edge of Cranborne Chase, is one such place, Buttermere on the Wiltshire–Hampshire border is another, while Dummer in Hampshire is a third. In each of these the church stands on the edge of the village, suggesting that a settlement was there well before Christianity arrived.

To see how valleys attracted the Anglo-Saxons it is merely necessary to glance at Ordnance Survey maps. Thus, the Salisbury Plain map shows concentrations of villages down the rivers which converge on Salisbury. The Wylye valley has twenty villages or hamlets within the eighteen miles from Warminster to Wilton, the Avon more than a dozen in a similar distance, while the Nadder and Ebble are equally well filled. Very often, settlements occur in pairs, one on each side of the river, all the way down the valley, while the upland ridges between valleys had a common frontier along the crests. The fair-minded Saxon farmers, recognizing the varying quality of land between riverside meadows and chalk hills, saw to it that each settlement had a fair share of each type. Today's parishes retain this pattern, being narrow along their river boundary, and elongated up to the downland ridge.

Reorganization of local government may have changed some administrative boundaries, but over much of Wessex the extent of parishes had been defined during the centuries of Anglo-Saxon settlement. Within the early parishes simple churches would have been built, most of which have been replaced more than once. Sometimes a preaching-cross would have sufficed, and some of these have survived, usually in a changed form. At Melbury Bubb the beautifully carved cross-shaft has been converted into the font; Codford St Peter, in the Wylye valley, has a small, carved cross-shaft of the ninth century, while Yetminster has a tenth-century one. The name Yetminster is a reminder that one way in which Christianity spread was by the setting-up of 'minster' churches, some being small monasteries, but others staffed by secular priests who lived in a community. Dorset has a number of such places.

Silver birches at Washer's Pit, near Dorset's highest village, Ashmore, Cranborne Chase.

Sturminster, Beaminster, Charminster, and Yetminster, and Wiltshire has Warminster.

More than a century of peace was broken by the arrival of warring Vikings from the Scandinavian coasts. By the year 872 a series of raids and battles spanning two decades destroyed the ancient kingdoms of Northumbria, East Anglia, and Mercia, so that only a single English kingdom remained. Wessex had steadily been growing in strength and importance, but by 872, with all of England north of the Thames held by the Norsemen, even Wessex seemed doomed. But, as so often in England's story, the hour brought forth the man, a prince of the house of Wessex, Alfred, born at Wantage in 849, the youngest son of King Ethelwulf. In his early childhood he had been taken on a pilgrimage by his father to Rome, and its culture must have cast its magic spell, and imbued in the boy a great desire to restore learning to his fellow-men. He taught himself to read Latin, yet as he grew to manhood he found himself regularly fighting, with his elder brothers, the marauding Danes. They, each in their turn, were Kings of Wessex, and when in 871 Ethelred died and was buried at Wimborne, Alfred succeeded him, was crowned at Winchester, and from there set about trying to defend England's last Christian kingdom.

By paying a ransom, called danegeld, he bought an uneasy peace, but it lasted for five years. During that time, when the Danes were busy dividing out the rest of the country, Alfred reorganized the levies of his rural populations, laid the foundations of our first fleet, and prepared to do battle against the savage and heathen enemy. In 876 the Great Army, as the Danish forces were called, marched across Wessex, and attacked and occupied Wareham so that they could use it as a base from which to conquer Wessex from the south. Armies from the Continent joined it, but a storm off Swanage destroyed many of their vessels.

Alfred met the challenge by blockading Wareham on its landward side. Although the Danes could obtain supplies by sea, they

The 3-foot-high Blowing Stone at Kingston Lisle, Berkshire, said to have been used to summon Alfred's army. The holes in the stone, when blown through, emit an eerie sound.

were impatient because they could not carry out their normal summer plundering of the countryside, so this time they requested a truce, paid danegeld to Alfred, and agreed to leave Wessex. But they broke their word, broke out of Wareham and headed westwards to Exeter, from where they ransacked Devon. Alfred followed and harried them to such an extent that eventually, in 877, the Danes were forced to withdraw their Great Army to Gloucester, just across the Mercian border. They did not like being defeated, and in the middle of winter, 877–78, under their great leader King Guthrum, moved southwards once more into Wessex, where they stockaded themselves in a strong defensive position by the River Avon at Chippenham, in Wiltshire. At the same time, a Danish fleet attacked the Devon coast, shattering the Wessex morale, so that some of Alfred's men fled to France. Alfred himself was forced to seek refuge in the marshlands of Somerset, on the lake isle of Athelney. He later told of his few months there, including the story of his burning the cakes at a cowherd's cottage. In 1693 a gold and enamelled jewel was found at Athelney, bearing the inscription *Aelfred Mea Hecht Gewyrean* – 'Alfred ordered me to be made'. This is now owned by Oxford University.

Once again this kind and scholarly leader bravely sought to rally his supporters. From the marshes of the River Parrett he sent messengers along the ancient Wessex tracks, ordering his followers to meet him. Six weeks after Easter 878, groups of men marched from Hampshire, Wiltshire and Somerset, but oddly enough, not Dorset, secretly through the fields and woods and by ancient trackways, converging at a place called Egbert's Stone on the chalk downs to the east of Selwood Forest, where Alfred met them. There is no sign of Egbert's Stone today, but it is thought to be near where Wiltshire, Somerset and Dorset meet, which would place it between Bourton and Zeals, to the south of Stourhead. My own fancy, unsupported by any evidence of an historical nature, puts this important meeting place close to the position of Alfred's Tower, on the northern edge of the Stourhead estates. The road

Alfred's Tower at Stourton, Wiltshire, built in 1772 to commemorate the King's victory over the Danes in the ninth century.

from the west follows the line of a very ancient track known as the Harroway (Hard Way on the O.S. map), one branch of which comes from Sherborne, by way of Yeovil and Cadbury Castle. Other ancient routes join it near Castle Cary, and where it climbs to the Wiltshire–Somerset border it is known as Kingsettle Hill, a hint from folk-memory, perhaps, of an old royal association. At the top of the hill, hidden in undergrowth, is the base socket of a cross, right on the county boundary yet not marked on the map.

The Danish army was about thirty miles away to the north. Alfred took his men towards them, camping for a night at a place called Icglea, which I suspect was Cley Hill, to the west of Warminster, whose isolated position would have made it an excellent look-out point. King's Bottom, a hollow on the northern edge of Longleat's estates, and close to Cley Hill, is another suggestive name. According to old chronicles, Alfred's men met the Danes at Ethandun, in today's language, Edington. But whether it is Edington at the foot of the Wiltshire Downs, or Edington, near Cheddar, is not apparent. Strong arguments support the claims of each, with the evidence of Bishop Asser, friend and biographer of Alfred, tilting the balance in favour of Edington on the Polden Hills.

In any event Alfred's army was victorious; they pursued, harried and beleaguered the Danes, who eventually capitulated. His greatness asserted itself to the full. He not only fed the enemy forces, and offered them peace, but showed magnanimity, and invited the Danish King Guthrum to accept Christian baptism. Alfred stood godfather to him. The Peace of Wedmore was a turning-point in our history, making it possible for Danes and Anglo-Saxons to live together peacefully. Recognizing that more Danish forces could always invade our shores, Alfred used the hard-won peace thoroughly to reorganize the English army, to build more ships and to create fortified towns or burghs. These strongholds would be permanently garrisoned, and if attacked, could probably hold out until his own mobile field army could destroy the enemy invaders. Thus, by the end of Alfred's reign many defensive centres had been set up throughout Wessex, their valorous burghers the seasoned veterans of Alfred's many battles. These small towns were the beginnings of urban life in England, sentinels against the Vikings.

Part of the Pilgrims' School at Winchester.

Some of these, like Alfred's capital of Wessex, Winchester, and Dorchester, occupied the sites, and often used the stones, of Roman towns before them. Others, like Newbury, Westbury, Bridport, and Shaftesbury, were new creations. At Wareham, the Saxon defences still survive as earthen embankments round three sides of the town, the River Frome guarding the southern approach. The road from the north gives the most impressive aspect of the original Saxon defences.

There had been a Saxon cathedral at Winchester before the end of the seventh century, and it was in 852 that Bishop Swithun became head of the diocese, and in addition to his normal episcopal duties, he fortified the cathedral, so that it withstood later attack, by the Danes, and he also tutored the young Alfred.

69

There is a peculiar irony in the fact that it was he who inspired the love of learning in the future king, who in turn desired the arts of peace, and he also seems responsible for forty days' rain after 16 July! Winchester became Alfred's capital, the centre of his administration, and the nascent point from which sprang a great religious revival. For not only did Alfred fortify twenty-five towns, and employ foreign scholars to raise the standard of Wessex culture, but he also imported monks from abroad. He restored old monasteries such as Wimborne and founded new ones, including those at Athelney and Shaftesbury. His enthusiasm for education created a uniquely literate lay nobility, so that no longer was it only priests and holy clerks who could read. He had taught himself this basic skill to such an extent that he was able to translate into a rather vernacular Saxon language the more useful Latin writings of Christian and classical literature, something which no one had done before. He was also responsible for starting the first history of the English people, written in their own language. No nation in Western Europe can match the Anglo-Saxon Chronicle, written by monks, and continued for two centuries after Alfred's death, at the age of fifty, in 899. His greatest legacies were a kingdom to which all Englishmen belonged, and a native literary culture.

Wessex is proud of Alfred. Many of its towns have their Alfred Street, just as a few villages seem to recognize the enemy defeated, by having fields or lanes called Danesfield, Danes' Bottom, Danes' Ditch, Danes' View. Ask local inhabitants for reasons and you will be told "Oh, that's where the Danes were beaten", or "The Danes camped there". Eleven centuries may distort it, but folk-memory is an aspect of Wessex history not easily overlooked. Alfred, however, looks over at least three places in Wessex, Winchester, Wantage and Pewsey, but none of the statues is very old, and in none of them does he look particularly happy with what he sees. This is scarcely surprising, since cathedral city, market town, and small country town have suffered at the hands of twentieth-century non-

Winchester: the fourteenth-century east face of the west gate, a former boundary of the medieval city.

71

An example of the strip lynchets of Anglo-Saxon agriculture, at
Sherrington in the Wylye valley, Wiltshire.

culture. Oh, that Alfred were alive today to fight the power of planners' sway!

Many features of the Wessex landscape which we can see today have come down to us from Anglo-Saxon times. The heavy plough used by Saxon farmers to win marginal land on the hill slopes of the downs on which to grow corn for the growing population produced horizontal terraces called strip-lynchets. These frequently occur in series, or flights, consisting of five or six parallel bands on a hillside. Good examples occur all over the Wessex uplands, easy to identify. Bishopstone, near Swindon, Sherrington in the Wylye valley, at Mere, on some of the hills round Cadbury, by the coast at Worth Matravers, on the Isle of Portland, and at Abbotsbury, all show these cultivation terraces. Many of them seem to be about a furlong in length and a chain wide, giving a level area of an acre.

But it was not a plough but the toil of hundreds of pairs of

Glastonbury Tor, Somerset, from the north, shows lynchets along the hillside.

human hands using simple implements which created the largest linear earthwork in southern England. The Wansdyke stretches for almost forty miles from east of Marlborough to the hillfort of Maes Knoll, on the Mendip Hills. Probably built in the sixth century by the Britons in the west as a defence against Saxon attacks from the north, it consists of a huge ditch, with banks on each side. Although much of it is now obscured by woodlands and later roads, a fine section of a dozen miles or so extends across the

Wansdyke, near Devizes, Wiltshire — a seventh- or eighth-century earthwork snaking its way across the downs.

Wiltshire Downs north of Pewsey Vale, exhilarating walking on a fresh, spring day, beneath lark song and April skies, lambs' voices and the wind in the grass. Motorists catch a glimpse of Wansdyke at Shepherd's Shore, on the Beckhampton–Devizes road, showing the earthwork snaking up to the crest of Morgan's Hill. Better still, Wiltshire County Council have created a small picnic site by Smallgrain Plantation to the west of Morgan's Hill, on the Calne road, with easy access to the Wansdyke, and fine views along it from the top of the hill, where, for a short distance, the Roman road from London to Bath follows the alignment of Wansdyke.

Over 900 feet up on the Wiltshire Downs, above Alton Barnes in the Vale of Pewsey, Orna Mere must be one of the most ancient dew-ponds in England. Anglo-Saxon land charters of the ninth century refer to it by name, and the fact that a present parish

Orna Mere dew-pond above Alton Barnes, Wiltshire, mentioned in an Anglo-Saxon land charter.

boundary passes through it is one more proof of the antiquity of many of our boundaries. Another charter of 825 refers to an un- usual stone on the boundary of Alton Priors parish; this has been rediscovered in its original position. Large Anglo-Saxon estates defined their boundaries very often by large banks and ditches. Sometimes where two adjoining estates each made a boundary bank, the common ditch ran between them. Over the course of centuries this has occasionally been used as a trackway, and may now have a sunken lane running along it. Where there seems to be no logical reason for such a 'hollow way', say that of linking vil- lages, it may well be an ancient boundary.

Wessex has a number of such surprises. To the north and north- north-west of Somerton, close to the Somerset fenlands, there is such a boundary-bank, with a lane this time following the top of one of its banks, along the edge of what was once a royal estate. Alongside the Harroway, already referred to, eastwards from the top of Kingsettle Hill, the road is bordered by an embanked hollow, with beeches growing along the ridges, with a slight hollow between, which is the boundary between two Saxon parishes of Kilmington and Stourton.

The names of Wessex villages indicate how Anglo-Saxon settlement spread throughout the whole area. As we drive through the -tons, -leys, -hams, and -burys we are going through places which have been continuously inhabited for more than a thousand years. With fire, axe, mattock and spade, our ancestors cleared the forests and woodlands, found suitable water supplies, built simple wooden houses, tilled the soil and tended their stock, living out their brief lives in small communities, under a simple if rough justice, and the beginnings of law. Successive Saxon kings continued to encourage the founding of monasteries. Alfred's grandson, King Athelstan, who had extended England's unity far beyond the old boundaries of Wessex, founded Milton Abbey in Dorset, and his younger brother and successor, King Edmund, appointed a monk, Dunstan, to be abbot of the revived monastery at Glastonbury. This soon became famous as a centre for music, the teaching of the Gospel, and its fine services. In 960 Dunstan became Archbishop of Canterbury, and together with Ethelwold, Bishop of Winchester, and Oswald, Bishop of York, was largely responsible for reviving Benedictine rule in its original form, at most monasteries, including Bath, Cerne, Westbury, Cranborne, Sherborne, Winchester and Glastonbury itself.

It was at Bath Abbey in 973 that Alfred's great-grandson, Edgar, was crowned first king of all England. The earliest form of the service still used at coronations was read by Archbishop Dunstan, who had prepared it. Behind its solemn rituals, consecration, anointing and investiture, together with the anthem 'Zadok the Priest' linking Saxon kings with distant Hebrews, is the theme of the anointed sovereign and his subjects. Thus under a Wessex king and a Wessex monk did another of the strongest English institutions come into being, Wessex became the cultural centre of the new kingdom, and Winchester was its capital.

During the reigns of Athelstan and Edgar, in the tenth century, Anglo-Saxon art and craftsmanship enjoyed a new flowering. The sculptured angels at St Lawrence, Bradford-on-Avon, a little-known Virgin and Child in the beautiful church at Inglesham, by the upper Thames, opposite Lechlade, an archway at Britford, south of Salisbury, two coped stones at Ramsbury, are some Saxon offerings from Wiltshire. Dorset shows us St Mary, Wareham, carvings at Stinsford and Winterborne Steepleton, while Sherborne Abbey's west front reveals in its rougher masonry and shafts some of the original Saxon church. In Hampshire, recent excavations to the north of the present nave of Winchester Cathedral have brought to light part of the old minster, founded in the seventh century but rebuilt between 971 and 994. A new minster, started in 903 alongside the old, remains to be excavated. At these two Anglo-Saxon buildings were crowned and buried many of the kings of Wessex and England. Tombchests of some of these are on the south side of the chancel of the present cathedral, including that of Alfred's father, Ethelwulf, and the Danish Canute, with his wife Emma. Of later Saxon times, that is about 1000, there are famous carvings at Romsey Abbey, where an impressive rood adorns the outside wall of the south transept, and at Headbourne Worthy, where the remarkable Crucifixion group, of Christ, the Virgin and St John, more than life-size, but vandalized. However, the Christ here, as at Romsey, has the Hand of God above Him, appearing, as it were, out of a cloud. In the far west of Hampshire, almost on the Wiltshire border, Breamore church is the best of all the county's Anglo-Saxon survivals, with an inscription round its south transept arch: HER SPUTELAD SEO GECPYDRAEDNEC DE (Here the covenant is explained to thee).

After Edgar died in 975, strife followed, as a result of the murder of one of his sons, Edward, at Corfe Castle, and the succession to the throne of Edward's half-brother, Ethelred, a spoilt and weak young man. Violence and unrest in a divided country encouraged more invasions by the Danes, and in 998 the new hordes had plundered their way into Wessex. For almost two decades England was helpless, monasteries were ransacked, peasants on the farms and in the villages were taxed to starvation or sold as slaves. In 1013 Ethelred fled to France, and four years later Cnut, or Canute, became King of England, and, accepting the Christian crown, agreed to govern his realm by the old laws of Edgar.

Cnut died in 1035, followed seven years later by the last of his sons. The pious, peace-seeking Edward, Ethelred's son, was chosen as his successor, but more squabbles occurred over the next thirty years, and after Edward's death in January 1066, Harold, Earl of Wessex, was chosen to be king. In October that same year, he led the English armies against the new invader, William, from France, and at Hastings he was defeated. Together with the thanes and earls of Wessex, and many men of a fine army, he died. The House of Wessex was ended. But as we have seen, the land of Wessex was good farmland, six centuries of Anglo-Saxon settlement had laid the pattern of villages and farms, of small towns, and cathedral centres, of great estates, royal, monastic and lay. Life had to continue even if there were changes at the top. Season followed season, harvest succeeded spring, and within the framework of village and shire, England was the richest and most fairly administered kingdom in Western Europe.

By the time of the great Domesday Survey of 1086, much of Wessex was still regarded as waste, perhaps as much as a quarter of the whole area. Taken as a whole, the population of England was about 1½ million, of which one-tenth lived in towns and boroughs. Hampshire and Wiltshire are estimated to have had 40,000–50,000 people, Dorset just under 40,000, and the whole of Somerset over 50,000. The Wessex of this book certainly had fewer than 15 people per square mile, as little as 5 in some areas of heathland and poor soils. Like the rest of the country it was grossly underpopulated, yet almost every Wessex village we know today was on the scene, many with their churches, and those in the river valleys having mills.

Monasteries and churches were the biggest landowners, possibly accounting for as much as a third of all the estates in Wessex. The nunnery at Shaftesbury, the largest in England, owned huge estates in Dorset and Wiltshire, while the other Benedictine abbeys owned thousands of acres of downland sheep walks. What was not

The foundations of the Norman cathedral at Old Sarum. Populated since the Iron Age, Old Sarum was deserted in the early thirteenth century for New Sarum, two miles away.

owned by the churches was under the control of the King, and his two hundred barons and six thousand knights, many of whose Norman names were subsequently added to those of the original Saxon villages where they acquired manorial estates, giving us the delightful double-barrelled euphony which makes map-reading a delight but signposting an expense. Charlton Mackrell, Keinton Mandeville, Broughton Gifford, Stanton St Quentin, Wootton Fitzpaine, Litton Cheney, Worth Matravers, Hurstbourne Tarrant, Shepton Mallet represent a fair sample. This last name is a reminder of the importance of sheep, it was the 'sheep town'. It has been calculated that at the time of the Domesday Survey there were about $7\frac{1}{2}$ million sheep in England, five for every single inhabitant. The chalk downlands of Wessex provided good grazing for the thousands of sheep owned by the monastic and other estates. Glastonbury and Shaftesbury Abbeys numbered their flocks in tens of thousands, while the Bishop of Winchester had even more. By the beginning of Norman times the foundations of medieval sheep-farming and its resultant wool trade prosperity had already been laid.

A view of Domesday Wessex does not show merely the sheep on the chalk. They were but one element in a mixed husbandry which prevailed across the whole of the belt of Midland England extending from the Wessex coast to Lincolnshire and North Yorkshire. Each village was surrounded by its own territory farmed on a community basis. Village sizes varied, from perhaps 20 to 120 inhabitants, say 4 to 30 households occupied by peasant farmers and their families. They were concerned with utilizing the arable land, grazing riverside meadows and permanent pastures, and exploiting the natural resources of woods, forests, fens and rivers. The village arable land was divided into three main fields, one with winter crops, one with spring crops, and one fallow. Between seed-time and harvest temporary fences protected the crops, but after harvest these were removed and the village stock allowed to graze the stubble – and manure the ground. Within the main fields, peasants had their individual strips, not all in one batch, but scattered. They also had their sheep, folded on the strips of fallow in the open fields, and a single village may have had as many as two

*Tisbury, south Wiltshire: the 200-foot-long Tithe Barn at Place Farm
was once a grange of Shaftesbury Abbey. Its recently re-thatched roof
contains about 1,450 square yards of thatching.*

or three thousand.

Of the houses in which they lived nothing remains today. At the
other end of the social scale, however, Wessex retains a few
examples of castles built during Norman times, although time has
treated most of them quite harshly. A number of motte and bailey
earthworks are evidence of simple fortresses for Norman nobles or
knights, and sometimes for the King. William built a castle at
Marlborough, and its motte is a prominent feature in the grounds

of the college. At Old Sarum, the great earthworks motte in the middle of the Iron Age hillfort was built, and a stronger stone structure added early in the twelfth century by the great Baron-Bishop Roger of Salisbury, who was also responsible for the Old Castle at Sherborne in Dorset. These two fortress-palaces were unique in Europe at that time, having not a strongly fortified keep, but a main building surrounded by a cloistered range forming a quadrangle. Remains at Sherborne are fragmentary, at Old Sarum none above ground, but what does survive, coupled with what has been revealed by excavations, indicates that these two structures were years ahead of their time, in plan and design.

Bishop Roger also built Devizes Castle, to the west of the town, on the site of an earlier motte and bailey. It lasted until the Civil War, and in 1842 a castellated replacement successfully hid any traces of the original building. However, the attractively curved outline of Devizes Market Place marks the shape of the outer bailey of Roger's castle. It is sad that we cannot today enjoy the sight of what Leland described as having "divers goodly towers", with a main hall 70 feet long. In the north of Wiltshire, the same Bishop Roger built Malmesbury Castle, which was dismantled in 1216 to provide stone for the abbey. The Castle Hotel now occupies the old site. Sherrington, a beautiful village in the Wylye valley, has its motte and bailey near the church, and now forming an island in a tree-fringed pond of unusually clear water. At the eastern end of Wiltshire near Andover, extensive earthworks and a few flint walls are all that survive of the royal castle at Ludgershall. The neighbouring county of Hampshire is not rich in castles. Pride of place must go to the superb keep at Portchester, and the curtain-walls of its inner bailey, contributing to its importance as a royal fortress particularly associated with military movements through Portsmouth, which began to grow during the twelfth and thirteenth centuries. By comparison, the Norman remains of the fortress-palaces of the Bishops of Winchester, Wolvesey, within the cathedral precinct, and at Bishop's Waltham, are meagre indeed. On the Isle of Wight the only extensive castle is Carisbrooke, where the distant view shows low buildings on a hill; on its motte is the Norman shell keep, with a low curtain wall below

Corfe Castle, Dorset, from the north.

it, and angle towers added to it in later years.

Finally in Dorset, apart from Sherborne Old Castle, motte and bailey earthworks survive in good condition at Powerstock, Cranborne, and Christchurch, where a bowling-green separates the huge mound from the Constable's House of 1160. On the eastern cliff-edge of the Isle of Portland, above Church Ope Cove, and visible from the footpath between the beach and cliffs, Rufus Castle was built in the twelfth century, probably to protect the royal manor of Portland. Corfe has Dorset's best-known and most extensive castle, its natural hill-top motte commanding the only gap in the chalk ridge which gave access to the Isle of Purbeck. It gives us a classic example of a Norman tower-keep subsequently reinforced by curtain walls and bastions, impregnable until the development of weapons strong enough to shatter it from the nearby

*Winterborne Tomson church, near Blandford, Dorset, is a rare survival of
an early medieval church unaltered by re-building. It was restored in 1931.*

ridges. There may well have been a pre-Conquest fortress at
Corfe, but it was during the two centuries of royal ownership after
the Conquest that it grew to greatness. Henry III made it a royal
palace; in Edward IV's reign the unfortunate Duke of Clarence
owned it, and later Protector Somerset. Passing to the Hattons
during Elizabethan days, it was sold to Sir John Bankes in 1635.
During the Civil War it was severely damaged, and after long
resisting parliamentary forces, the great keep was eventually
undermined and shattered by explosives. Now, the glorious disarray of its masonry enhances the grandeur of its silhouette against
the smooth Dorset skyline.

The Norman castles of Wessex reveal in the ruined fragments
only a hint of the new powers which dominated the physical scene.
Similarly, from a spiritual point of view, towers of newly built
Norman churches rose above towns and villages, a challenge and a
proud proclamation of the Faith. Yet again, only parts of these

Norman buildings remain, for as with most churches, great and small, changes, additions, remodellings and sometimes complete rebuildings, over the succeeding four or five centuries, have either replaced or obscured much of the original Norman work.

Impressive as are the various Norman parts of the great churches – Winchester Cathedral (especially the crypt and transepts), Christchurch Priory, and the abbey churches of Romsey, Wimborne, Sherborne and Malmesbury, it is the smaller village churches which I find most appealing. Studland, in the heathlands of south-east Dorset, is one of the few almost complete Norman village churches in England, and Winterborne Tomson another, a little-known gem off the beaten track a few miles north-west of Bere Regis. Similarly rustic in its Wiltshire setting in the Vale of Pewsey, Manningford Bruce is also a complete little Norman building with nave, chancel and rounded apse, while the Romanesque architecture of St Mary, Portchester, in the south-east corner of the outer bailey of the castle, retains magnificent detail, particularly in its west front. Altogether grander with their mighty Norman crossing towers are the churches at East Meon, Hampshire, St John Devizes, in Wiltshire, and Milborne Port in south-east Somerset. The towns on to which these Norman towers looked down were small by present standards. Winchester, its capital, probably had fewer than 4,000 inhabitants, Old Sarum, Bath, Dorchester, Wareham, Shaftesbury and the other boroughs no more than 1,000 each. Some places that we think of as historic had not yet appeared on the Wessex scene – at the end of the eleventh century there was no Portsmouth or Salisbury, Weymouth or Poole, while Newbury was first mentioned only in 1080, and Swindon was no more than a hamlet.

Over huge areas of the countryside there were great tracts of marshland, heath and woodland waiting to be reclaimed, a process which was to occupy an immense amount of pioneering activity over the next three centuries. Beechwoods extended over many square miles of the chalk uplands, and in the clay vales, although some clearances had been made, thousands of oak and ash trees dominated dense woodland, while elm, maple and lime were also very common. Frontiers of settlement did not extend very far from

Above: *A Norman doorway in Romsey Abbey.*

Opposite: *Christchurch Priory, Hampshire – a Norman turret in the
north transept.*

the homesteads of each village, and much of Wessex remained 'forest' in a sense other than woodland. It was countryside, both wooded and open, set aside as hunting preserve, for the King or his nobles, and subject to special law – forest law. Cranborne Chase, Selwood Forest, Powerstock and Micheldever were such forests, now very much diminished; Savernake, south of Marlborough, still shows its forest character though not so well as the more famous New Forest in Hampshire, the oldest of England's forests, but new for William the Conqueror who created it.

St. Mary's Uffington, Berkshire: a large cruciform church of c.1250, *with an octagonal top storey on the square tower.*

CHAPTER 3

TOWNS AND TRADE

APART FROM the quality of the countryside itself much of the unique character of Wessex is to be found in its country towns. Many of them have their roots, as we have seen, in Anglo-Saxon times, a few, like Winchester, Dorchester and Bath, boasting a Roman ancestry. During the period from 1066 to 1346, the time of the Black Death, hundreds of new towns sprang up all over England, mainly as a result of lords of various manors – royal, monastic, church and lay landowners – seeking to increase their revenues by encouraging the establishment of towns on their lands. In addition, many villages acquired market charters, and with them, frequently, town status, while towns already in existence began to grow more rapidly. Wessex had its share of this urban expansion, and it would be no exaggeration to say that market places proliferated over the whole region, as much as car parking areas do today.

Both new towns and old-established ones acquired their inhabitants not only from natural growth in population, but also by attracting people from the surrounding countryside. Certainly by

Seventeenth-century weavers' houses at Corsham, Wiltshire.

Above: *Bradford-on-Avon, Wiltshire — a Saxon settlement at the broad ford, spanned by a fourteenth-century bridge widened in the seventeenth century when the lock-up (left) was added.*

Opposite: *The George Inn at Norton St Philip near Bath, one of England's most remarkable medieval inns, built probably by nearby Hinton Priory as a staple for the wool produced on its estates on the northern edge of Selwood Forest.*

the end of the thirteenth century some areas of England, including parts of Wessex, were becoming almost over-populated, so that there could be a justifiable movement to towns. Most of these towns survive today, facets of their own individuality still managing to peep out, if only wanly, from their all-too-familiar cloak of modern development, new housing estates, and fast bypass roads, which combine with hideous efficiency to make each town more and more like every other one. Generally speaking, the larger a town grows, the less it retains its personality, and more are the layers of shrouding mish-mash which have to be penetrated to reach the ancient heart.

Happily there is only a handful of big towns in Wessex, and I propose to leave those until the end of this chapter. For now I want to suggest that the only way to enjoy, appreciate and understand small towns is on foot. A car is an insulation against history as much as it is against nature, but on foot you may see lengths of Roman walling, Saxon earthworks, monastic and castle remains, market crosses, the names of streets, inn signs, medieval churches, in short that indefinable patina which time bestows on one place, making it different from another. As you walk the streets, including those which go behind the houses and shops, you soon become eager to find answers to the questions: why is the town here, how and why (or why not) has it grown, where is its nucleus?

Much of my own exploration of Wessex towns has inevitably been done at weekends. In one respect, a Sunday is a good day, for the streets are usually less busy, making walking both quieter and safer. Recently, however, a factor has emerged to destroy some of this peaceful atmosphere. Modern youth (I am being polite), monied, motor-cycled and bored, meets in market places and High Streets, and seems to spend its Sunday afternoons roaring round the centres of Wimborne, Blandford, Devizes, Westbury, Salisbury. The towns of Wessex are obviously dead for them. Saturdays are not much better, for those same characters then have more people to annoy. I'm sure they succeed. But the main fault of Sunday explorations is that the essential life of the towns is missing. Market towns grew because they fulfilled the needs of trade within their own locality. They may not have the same influence now,

Somerton market-place and seventeenth-century market-cross.

but it is on market-days that most of these Wessex towns show the best side of their characters. Folk still come in from the surrounding countryside, not necessarily to trade, not even to shop, but because, perhaps, they have an instinctive recognition that by so doing they are ensuring the security of a continuing theme. Monday at Sturminster Newton, Wednesday at New Alresford, Tuesday at Wantage, Saturday at Sherborne, and so on.

This continuity of a way of life in market towns is one of their main fascinations. In their market-squares, around their market-crosses, generations of people have bought and sold goods and produce. Sometimes, nearby, a lock-up, stocks or whipping-post have held their wrong-doers; fairs have taken place in large market-places, ancient rights still proudly maintained, on saints' days, feast days, and hirings, reminders that the market is part of our way of life. Wessex being primarily a farming region, its market towns have always had strong links with the land, although now the live-stock side of the market is usually held in a separate, purpose-built

structure, perhaps on the edge of the town. Some market towns have kept more of their history and ancestry than others, but all have something worth seeking and worth seeing, even if it is only a glimpse of a way of life which, in the stressful conditions of today, might almost be envied.

There was more movement among the people of thirteenth- and fourteenth-century Wessex than is generally realized. Even medieval villages were not isolated communities; peasants as well as farmers transported produce over short distances, and were partly responsible for the growth of markets, which relied on this short-range exchange of goods. Generally speaking, market towns operated quite successfully within a sphere of influence of five or six miles at most. When charters were granted, at neighbouring markets, they usually specified different market days. Itinerant traders and merchants would frequent a group of four or five markets each on a different day of the week, a system which still applies in many areas of Wessex today.

Villages carried their own basic trades – bakers, brewers, carpenters, cobblers and smiths; less common trades were provided by the towns – butchers, weavers, dyers, tailors, shoemakers, tanners, millers, farriers and perhaps a spicer, a locksmith, a glover, a barber, a shearer. Goods produced only in certain areas of the country and distributed for sale all over were brought to the market towns. Salt from Worcestershire, Cheshire and various coastal saltpans; metals, grain, furs, wine – imported, these last two – found their way by slow stages to the rural population. All these goods were carried to and from the markets either in sacks on the backs of packhorses (2$\frac{1}{2}$ hundredweight per animal), or on carts; journeys would be long, tedious and uncomfortable, for as yet there was no road system linking towns and villages, just rough tracks. Today, good roads and the mobility which the car has brought make market towns easily accessible to people living in a wide area around them.

A new influx of dwellers has also come to the country towns of

Malmesbury: in the centre of the town stands this market-cross erected in about 1500.

97

Wessex. Scarcely anywhere in Hampshire or Wiltshire is more than an hour by road from a large town or city, while much of Dorset can almost be regarded as within commuting distance of Yeovil, Weymouth, Poole or Salisbury. Thus an increasing proportion of residents do not work in the towns of Wessex where they live, nor in the countryside around. They are more dependent on large industrial cities for many of the things they need, and as so many of these are either non-repairable, or made of plastic, there is little further need for service industries which used to be so vital a factor in local rural economy. Garages, agricultural engineers and builders are the important country town trades today.

Shops in the country towns still meet most of the needs of the local people, but it is noticeable how branches of multiple stores are ousting the old family businesses, so that fascias and window-dressings are becoming the same, sticker-advertisements the same, and of course the goods inside the same. Again, happily, pockets of individuality hold out against the tide of mediocracy, and old trade signs can be still found above some shops. The more a town has become a place full of 'des. res.' and generally bypassed by main roads and light industrial development, the more likely it is to have antique shops, craft shops and tea-rooms.

Most Wessex towns manage to fit into a pattern of country life usually envied by people who live in huge industrial areas. The further west you go the more does this sense of locality become apparent. The country towns of Dorset still seem to have closer links with the land than those of east and north-east Wessex. Physical background has always been an important factor in the siting of a town. Well chosen, and with good communications, a town is likely to flourish; without them it could easily fail. Nature would also play a part, especially with coastal towns, where the silting-up of estuaries and harbours was likely to spell doom for any settlement nearby. The shape and lay-out of towns, and the way they have grown, are dependent on their sites and on land ownership. Any view of Wessex towns should include samples of many different types.

The problem is, as always, one of selection. Should this be based on architectural merit, an historic past, a literary association, or merely good car parking facilities? One thing is reasonably certain, and that is that no town in Wessex – or in Britain for that matter – is more worth seeing than another were it not for what Sir John Summerson calls "the enormous, obstinate and overwhelming legacy of the past". Even the most ruthless Mammonic developer has not succeeded in obliterating all of this yet, although he has tried, and continues to try, hard. A town's character is very largely the result of this accumulated humus reflected in its layout, its buildings, its trades, its names. Within recent years legislation has helped to save a number of fine buildings; equally, amenity and civic societies have highlighted local problems and have undoubtedly been responsible for alerting authorities to their responsibilities towards preserving something of a town's heritage. County councils have designated numerous Conservation Areas, yet always I have the feeling that the enemy is at the gates.

Each town has a unique quality, even, if one may paraphrase Orwell, "some are more unique than others". In 1964 the Council for British Archaeology suggested that throughout Britain there were over 660 historic towns, of which about half justified careful treatment in respect of future planning and development. Of these, 232 were in England, but when this list is broken down, the Wessex counties fare rather badly. Dorset has nine names, Blandford, Bridport, Dorchester, Lyme Regis, Shaftesbury, Sherborne, Wareham, Weymouth and Wimborne. Hampshire's four towns were Lymington, Romsey, Southampton, Winchester, with Ryde the only representative of the Isle of Wight. Somerset's contribution was Bath, Bruton, Somerton and Wells, while from Wiltshire came Bradford-on-Avon, Corsham, Devizes, Malmesbury, Marlborough, Salisbury and Wilton. Twenty-five altogether, from which in a separate list of fifty-one critically important 'gem' towns, Bath, Blandford, Bradford-on-Avon, Marlborough, Salisbury and Wells emerge as the Wessex frontrunners.

Rightly, the CBA were anxious to point out that their lists were not final, not even necessarily definitive, and that if some towns were omitted, it did not imply that they were not worth a second thought. Hampshire supporters could find justification for including New Alresford, Bishop's Waltham, Fareham, Odiham, Petersfield and Wickham (or is that a village?). Moonrakers would like to have Cricklade and Highworth, and from Somerset perhaps Frome might have scraped in — not now, though, for there the enemy has gained too strong a foothold.

Almost all the towns mentioned have three elements in common, a medieval nucleus, a Georgian development, and a Victorian perimeter, which, to visitors, is the part first seen. The bigger the town the thicker is this section, best left to be explored last. These three elements contribute to the town's character; housing estates from between the wars and post-1950 add nothing to it, but merely reduce it to a featureless modernistic norm. Swindon, in north Wiltshire, mushroomed from the 1840s, when Brunel drove his railway line to the west, established railway workshops near his new station, and built one of the first industrial housing areas in the country. The whole of Swindon's 'railway village' is now a Conservation Area, and is the best part of the town. Houses had a reason for being there, and the streets were planned. From that nucleus the spread of Swindon up the hill to the south, beyond the foot of the downs, is rather like a bad dream. Now that the M4 cuts its way across the countryside to the south, Swindon sits uneasily between the communicational Scylla and Charybdis of railway and road.

To find the heart of an old town you usually seek the church, the market-place, the High Street (or sometimes Broad Street, or just The Square or The Bury). If the church overlooks the market-place, or at least is very close to it, then somewhere in that area were usually the beginnings of that town. Usually, but not always. If the town had grown near a river-crossing the parish church may have been built a short distance away from that point, above any flood level of the river. I had lived near, and worked in, Bradford-on-Avon for many years before I discovered that it probably had two nuclei, one on the north side of the river near the medieval bridge, and the other some little distance to the west, beyond the Saxon church, at a spring still known as 'Ladywell' — itself a reminder that a town needed a good fresh-water supply, and the source of this is another pointer to the siting of a town. Church

Railway company houses in Bathampton Street, Swindon, built in the 1850s of stone from Box Tunnel.

Street – also another old name to look for – runs from near the town bridge to the parish church, and must have been one of the oldest streets in Bradford. The fact that most of its remaining buildings were re-fronted in Georgian times, with older parts hidden from view, illustrates again how, once a street pattern of houses has been established, it does not change much, but undergoes successive rebuildings, and infillings.

Like most medieval towns in Wessex, Bradford is organic, that is, like Topsy it simply grew. The usual form of a town was as a thoroughfare, consisting of one long street, with houses on each side. Alton, Lyndhurst, Melksham, Odiham and Warminster are all examples of this basic form. Alton, Melksham and Odiham each have their fine parish churches lying just off the High Street, reached by a short road, and on slightly higher ground. In the case of Odiham, the church adjoins a small open square, The Bury. Melksham's main street widens out into the market-place, while at Marlborough the whole High Street is immensely broad, the result of its having been one of the most important markets for sheep from the surrounding Wiltshire Downs. No doubt in medieval times you could expect to see anything up to 10,000 sheep there. Today, at weekends, you feel there is the same number of vehicles. New Alresford, Bridport, Dorchester, Fareham and Malmesbury have two main streets meeting at right-angles, with the market occupying a site near the junction. This also happens at Sherborne where, as though to emphasize its nucleus, the Conduit stands in the little market area, almost within the shadow of the great abbey church.

It is difficult to imagine an English country town without its church, a memory-bank of life and death, talk and trade, prayer and pageant. Norman, Early English, Decorated and Perpendicular, particularly the tower, represent an increasing prosperity through the Middle Ages, usually based on wool. Churches, castles, manor houses and tithe barns were the only buildings of the Middle Ages for which local materials need not necessarily have been used. For small houses and cottages wood was the commonest building material, but from the sixteenth and seventeenth centuries brick and stone, where good quarries existed, superseded it. But because most of a town's buildings were of timber, fires frequently occurred, sometimes with devastating results.

In 1731 almost the whole of Blandford was destroyed, with the loss of the parish church and 400 houses. Almost immediately two local architect-brothers, John and William Bastard, were given the responsibility of rebuilding it; by 1760 the job was finished, so what we see today is an extraordinarily harmonious piece of Georgian townscape combining a consistent use of brick and tile, while still allowing individuality its head. Marlborough suffered similarly, its last major fire having been in 1653, and no thatched roofs were allowed after 1690. Most of present Marlborough, both along the High Street and up by The Green, is Georgian, but less consistently so than Blandford. Marlborough's High Street broadens at each end, where two

Beaminster, Dorset: one of a number of Wessex "minster" towns.

churches stand on near-island sites, the only encroachments into the huge space, except at the October Mop Fair.

Infilling of market-places was at its most active during the late thirteenth and early fourteenth centuries, because a rising population created demands on the limited urban space available. Later on, after visitations of various plagues reduced population, numbers continued to rise steadily again, so that infilling continued, sometimes in market places, more often along the main street, in seventeenth- and eighteenth-century ribbon development. Smaller houses were built behind, and often in the grounds of, larger ones, a process not unknown today. When this happened, the builder quite commonly put up one or two rows of small cottages, a narrow paved yard, with a tunnel-like access along what was the side-passage of the medieval or later large house. Look round Wessex towns and you will see examples of these, particularly where some local industry has developed from the late eighteenth century onwards, with a resultant demand for labour.

Occasionally an old industry has influenced the lay-out of a town. Bridport is the best Wessex example, and is still this country's main producer of netting, twines, cords and ropes. In other towns past trades are more often preserved in street-names; people carrying on the same trade or craft naturally tended to congregate in the same part of a town, since they did not fear competition but thought it far more practical that customers knew where to find them – Tanner Row, Silver Street, Cinnamon Lane, Butcher Row, Shambles, Sheep Street. Petersfield boasts a street called The Spain, probably a reference to Spanish merchants who visited it during wool-trading days.

Just as our own century with its vastly increasing mobility produced big changes in towns, so did the greater ease of travel which the coaching era introduced. Around 1650 a fifty-mile journey took two days; by the end of the century this was halved, and

Bridport, Dorset: a perfect late-eighteenth-century shop-front in East Street, with two bowed shop-windows and similar windows of the shopkeeper's apartment in the upper storey.

when Victoria came to the throne it was down to four hours. Red Rover, Regulator, Traveller, Defiance and the Exeter Telegraph rattled their way down the Exeter road from London, crossing the spine of Wessex on the way, 172 miles in 17 hours through Basingstoke, Whitchurch, Salisbury, Blandford, Dorchester, and Bridport the coaches went. Travellers needed accommodation, and horses had to be changed at least every ten miles. Old inns were enlarged, given tall dignified façades, sash windows, pillared porches and high arched entrances to yards and stables. In small towns along the coaching roads to Portsmouth, Southampton, Exeter and Bath these late Georgian fronts add their own character to personalities of places, elegant monuments to a new age of travel. Marlborough has a number of coaching inns, of which the Castle Inn is now one of the houses of the College. At Calne, along the Bath road, the Landsdowne Arms has a brewhouse and fine stables behind its very long front, dominated by an enormous barometer. Devizes was on an alternative route from Marlborough, and its famous Bear easily identified by a large bear above the porch. Thomas Lawrence, the great portrait painter, was the son of a former landlord of the Bear. On the Exeter road, White Hart Inns at Whitchurch and Salisbury were famous coaching houses, Blandford has the Red Lion, Greyhound and Crown, Dorchester the King's Arms and Antelope, while there is another Greyhound in Bridport.

When the railways came in the 1840s and 1850s, the coaching era came to an end. The buildings which it spawned fell into a temporary decline, eclipsed by the smaller, unpretentious Railway Inns near the stations which were built, often on the edge of the towns. Victorian terrace houses, the better ones with bay windows, the poorer ones of very cheap bricks, sprang up along Station Roads, to house workers either on the railways, or in new industries which the railways brought to towns. On the whole, however, Wessex has escaped the more ravaging effects of the Industrial Revolution, but has continued to base its prosperity on agriculture.

Nevertheless most small towns in Wessex reveal some evidence of local industries, many associated with textiles. Until the end of the eighteenth century, cottage industries flourished, west Wiltshire becoming one of the centres of the important West of England cloth trade. In the middle of the seventeenth century, the great clothier Paul Methuen invited Flemish weavers to the area, giving fresh impetus to the weaving of broadcloths. They settled in Corsham and Bradford-on-Avon; these and other towns in the Avon valley and that of its main tributary the Frome prospered, merchants built fine houses, and when the industry became mechanized, mills sprang up in towns and villages. Many survive at Bradford, now used for other purposes, while Dryden's four-storey antique warehouse by the river at Malmesbury was formerly a silk-mill.

Sherborne's silk-mill of 1810 is slightly later, and is still in use, as part of a synthetic fibre plant. Terrace houses nearby were built for its workers. Whitchurch, in Hampshire, possesses a most handsome three-storey silk-mill, complete with bell-tower and clock, and iron-framed windows. Originally using the River Test to provide motive power, this is now done by electricity, and the mill continues to produce silk. Wickham's Chesapeake Mill of 1820, a four-storey brick building with a wooden gantry over its centre bay, is so named because its internal timbers were taken from an American vessel of that name, captured in 1813.

When the cloth trade declined in the late eighteenth and early nineteenth centuries, other occupations gained in importance, often taking over the mill buildings. The manufacture of buttons, gloves and lace, although never on a large scale, maintained a tradition of industry in quiet places. Breweries and tanneries added their contribution, while Melksham in Wiltshire grew to become the headquarters of the enormous Avon Rubber Company. Bemerton, near Salisbury, had been an important paper-manufacturing centre since the middle of the sixteenth century, and a 'rag' mill at Slaughterford, near Chippenham, manufactured the 'stuff' which became paper. Hampshire's clear chalk streams also were suitable for making paper from old rags and ropes, and mills at Alton and Laverstoke both manufactured the paper for bank-notes.

These examples have been given merely to emphasize that in a region so basically orientated towards farming, industries have always had a part to play, and the buildings associated with them are significant features in small towns. The end of the eighteenth century saw a few canals constructed, the Andover, which linked the two arms of the Southampton and Salisbury Canal; the Basingstoke Canal, also opened in 1794, to link Basingstoke with the River Wey and London, and, most important, the Kennet and Avon. John Rennie designed this, arguably the most beautiful of all our canals, linking Newbury and Bath, giving a waterway route across the north of Wessex. Although parts of it are navigable, especially at its eastern end, it is still not possible to travel by water directly from the Thames to the Severn. Although an enormous amount of voluntary work has helped to restore a number of pounds in Wiltshire, there remains the problem of the wonderful flight of locks near Devizes, and an awkward section between Bath and Bradford-on-Avon, which contains two handsome aqueducts. Indeed, throughout its length the Kennet and Avon is noted for its architectural details, making even a towpath exploration a worthwhile endeavour.

Wessex may have escaped much of the Industrial Revolution, but it did not escape the railways. Between about 1845 and 1885 the railway network of Wessex was virtually complete, so that by the time of the agricultural depression the railways had made it possible for labourers to leave their home districts and seek work in big towns, or abroad. This was the beginning of the break-up of rural communities and old ties. On the other side of the coin, they created new jobs and made it possible to transport milk and other produce quickly out of Wessex to the bigger centres of population. Where railway lines passed through towns, they brought new life and activity; places which railways missed lost their earlier importance, and ceased to be towns in the modern sense. Cerne Abbas is probably the best example of this. The last stage-coach passed through it in 1855, and the railway never came, so that it became isolated. Now, the new transport revolution enables travellers to rediscover the quiet delights of a small country town, and thereby shatter its peace.

Shaftesbury is the highest hill-top town in southern England, but even by the late nineteenth century it was a mere shadow of its

Shaftesbury, Dorset: Gold Hill, with Blackmore Vale beyond.

former greatness. Hardy laments what Shaston has lost, "Vague imaginings of its Castle, its three mints, its magnificent apsidal Abbey . . . its twelve churches, its shrines, chantries, hospitals . . . all now ruthlessly swept away". The present century has all but completed the destruction, and all that seems to be left is the view across the 'Vale of Little Dairies' from the terrace walk of the abbey gardens where Jude Fawley waited for Sue Phillitson, and cobbled Gold Hill.

By contrast, Sherborne, once the capital of Wessex, is a show-piece, and knows it. Honey-coloured Ham stone, much warmer than Chilmark, of which much of Shaftesbury is built, glows in friendly welcome. Its cathedral served as church of the great Bene-dictine abbey until the Dissolution, when the townsfolk bought it for use as their parish church. Medieval market town, scholastic centre, with the dignity of a small cathedral city, and having some light industries, it is not surprising that Sherborne smiles in satis-faction at having attained the best of all worlds, without loss of character or liveliness, and without becoming a museum piece.

Dorchester: Judge Jeffreys' lodging in High West Street is one of only two half-timbered, early-seventeenth-century buildings surviving relatively intact in this town.

Wimborne Minster is less satisfactory, mainly because it is in the huge Bournemouth–Poole hinterland. Vast rashes of new houses savage the green countryside south of the River Stour between Oakley and Canford. Within the town is a confusion of generally unpretentious houses and modernized shop fronts. A medieval Priest's House is now a museum and the fine minster church has two competing towers. Of the three good bridges on the approaches to the town, Julian Bridge, on the west, is easily the best.

Wareham we have already met as one of the oldest of all our Saxon towns, but it deserves another, longer visit. Marshy ground all round has ensured that Wareham has not exploded outwards, and fire destroyed most of the town in 1762. Thus it is now a pleasant example of Georgian planning, on the Roman grid pattern, with streets intersecting at right angles. The Quay, by the River Frome, is Wareham's best corner, suitably blessed by St Mary's Church. At the opposite end of the town, inside the Saxon church of St Martin, is Eric Kennington's beautiful effigy of T. E. Lawrence, full-length in Arab dress, cold white stone conveying something of the enigmatic character of one of the most remarkable men of this century.

The best way into Dorchester is from the east, across Grey's Bridge. As you enter the town there is a marvellous view of High Street, the town's spine running gently upwards to Top o' Town. Half way along, South Street, or Cornhill, leads off at right angles, the junction being the centre of Dorchester. Between 1613 and 1775 the town suffered five serious fires, so very few buildings reveal Dorchester's pre-Georgian past. One that does is Napper's Mite, once almshouses of 1610, now a shopping arcade, a rather unusual transmogrification. Country town, county town, market town, Dorchester is Hardy's Casterbridge, and the people in its streets and inns, especially on Wednesdays and Saturdays, are twentieth-century counterparts of characters in the great Wessex novels. Hardy himself sits pensively in stone at Top o' Town, while Max Gate, the house he built for himself on the southern edge of Dorchester, is appropriately gloomy and withdrawn. The County Museum, a modern building in late Victorian Gothic, has a room devoted to Hardy relics and mementoes, as well as some

Milton Abbas, Dorset, built between 1771 and 1790.

good natural history, geological and archaeological material. On my last visit to Dorchester I was pleased to see that elms along some of the approach roads are still there. They were planted by French prisoners of the Napoleonic Wars in gratitude for kindness shown by local folk.

It is doubtful if a similar sentiment was felt by the people of Milton Abbas, once a prosperous little market town in central Dorset, dominated by a great Benedictine monastery. Even the Dissolution failed to diminish the town's local importance. But between 1771 and 1790, Viscount Milton not only diminished it, but demolished it completely, so that he could empark the land round his new house. It took almost twenty years to carry out the plan, but eventually the people of Milton Abbas were rehoused in a new, planned village half-a-mile away, while the old town lies buried beneath a few feet of chalky Dorset earth, now grassed over, but retaining in its mounds and hollows a surface memory of the lay-out of former High Street, Broad Street, and the plots of old houses.

This rise and fall of Wessex towns presents a series of fascinating stories. Corfe obviously developed as a castle town, but grew to medieval importance through the rise of the Purbeck marble workings nearby. Gaining its market in 1215 and a fair in 1246, it expanded southwards along two roads which met at the foot of its castle. Sixteenth- and seventeenth-century houses mark the continuing prosperity which followed the granting of borough status in 1576. A hundred years later quarrying had declined to nothing. Trade ceased, and later buildings were much inferior in quality. Now, its architectural appeal and nearness to the Purbeck coast make Corfe a tourist centre, and one of the most impressively placed of English towns.

Malmesbury, in north Wiltshire, was a Saxon town which developed around St Aldhelm's Abbey, above a loop of the River Avon. One of the great early historians, William of Malmesbury, was a monk there in the twelfth century, while it was one of his monastic brothers who, equipped with home-made wings, attempted to fly from the top of the abbey tower. His gliding descent covered 200 yards, after which he crashed, broke his legs, and was crippled for life. A local pub name commemorates the event.

The rebuilt Norman abbey had a central crossing tower, with a later spire equalling Salisbury's, but about 1530 the great tower collapsed, followed a few years later by the smaller west tower. Then came the Dissolution, when a local clothier, William Stumpe, bought the abbey, demolished the choir and Lady Chapel, and quickly used various monastic buildings as loom sheds. He gave the nave to the town for its parish church, so at least something was saved of one of the great European monasteries. Malmesbury has many good things which give it a Wessex flavour – a handsome market cross, High Street slightly curving and descending southwards to the river, with King's Wall leading off, and almshouses, incorporating a fragment of a twelfth-century hospital, nearby. A new bypass keeps through traffic at bay, so that

Malmesbury preserves some odour of sanctity from its quieter past.

Chippenham has lost its soul to traffic and industry. The coming of the railway though, accompanied by good associated bridges, tunnels, cuttings and embankments, encouraged new trade, accelerated by improved roads, with the A4 passing through the town centre. One good street remains, St Mary's, behind the parish church, to make Chippenham just worth a visit. To Calne, nearby, the railway only threw out a branch line, and it retains more of a country town atmosphere, especially when Harris's bacon factory is at full steam. The best corners are around The Strand, in the centre of the town, and along Church Street southwards to The Green, where Georgian houses surround a wide grassy triangle.

Trowbridge is now Wiltshire's county town, and vast new administrative buildings symbolize the glazed growth of bureaucratic power. In the town centre a fine parish church reminds us of an earlier power, and a walk round the formless pattern of streets reveals an unexpectedly high number of Georgian houses, reflecting wool prosperity of those times. Many have been taken over by commerce, which has ensured their preservation. A few early nineteenth-century mills and terraces of weavers' cottages are reminders that this corner of Wessex was not left behind in the Industrial Revolution, but modern developments in the centre of the town show characteristic tastelessness of the 1970s.

Wilton was once the capital of Wessex, and Saxon kings had a palace nearby. Alfred founded a Benedictine nunnery on the southern edge of the town, and Bishop Poore, of Old Sarum, had his eye on the abbey lands as the site for his new cathedral. The Abbess dashed his hopes, so New Sarum arose by the meadows of the Avon, and flourished as a medieval town. Wilton was too close to compete, so steadily declined. At the Dissolution the abbey was given by the King to William Herbert, first Earl of Pembroke, so Wilton House rose from the abbey ruins, and the Pembrokes have been there ever since. Wilton is now an unspectacular country town whose lay-out preserves the plan of the former nunnery; in the market-place, the old parish church is a ruin, but its chancel was restored by Robert Bingham, American Ambassador 1933–47, in memory of one of his ancestors, Bishop Bingham. The new church was built in 1843 by T. G. Wyatt, a masterpiece in Italianate Romanesque. But apart from this and Wilton House it is the Royal Carpet Factory which is prominent. Although the industry started in the seventeenth century, the main building dates from the late eighteenth century, a splendid structure sixteen bays long, of brick.

In Hampshire, Romsey should take pride of place although it is a place where performance scarcely matches up to promise. Robust masonry of the Norman abbey more than compensates for what has been lost of the Benedictine convent. The town paid £100 for the abbey church at the Dissolution, even in those days a knock-down price for a 250-feet long nave, 70 feet high, with many architectural treasures and fine monuments. In the vestry is the beautiful Romsey Psalter, and the deed of sale of the abbey, bearing Henry VIII's signature.

Romsey Abbey overlooks the market-place, roughly triangular, presided over by Lord Palmerston. Occasional good buildings rather than groupings catch the eye, and this 'bittiness' continues in other parts of the town, where late Georgian and Regency houses give touches of elegance. King John's Hunting Lodge of 1230 is one of the earliest surviving secular buildings in Wessex, but apart from this and the abbey, the inns of Romsey are as good as anything, mainly classically fronted, but sometimes hiding Tudor interiors. The White Horse, Tudor Rose, Dolphin and Bishop Blaise – he was the patron saint of woolcombers – all add distinction to the town. The same cannot be said for its peripheral housing estates.

The New Forest part of Hampshire has always been thinly populated, and lacking good building stone, so that its towns are architecturally undistinguished. Fordingbridge grew at an important crossing of the Avon, still spanned by a seven-arched medieval bridge. Augustus John lived in the town for many years, and his statue stands by the river bank. Lower down the river is Ringwood, a much more important market town which has managed to retain a number of attractive houses of which the eighteenth-century Old Manor House in Southampton Road is the best. In West Street, near the market-place, Monmouth House gained its name because the ill-fated Duke lodged there after his Sedgemoor defeat. Ringwood now thrives as a tourist and small shopping centre for trout-fishermen and New Forest enthusiasts. But it is Lyndhurst which is the capital of the Forest, a mainly one-street town dominated by a huge brick Victorian Gothic church containing glass by William Morris and Burne-Jones, and a fresco by Lord Leighton. In the churchyard is the grave of Mrs Hargreaves, who as Alice Liddell was the original of Lewis Carroll's timeless heroine of childhood. The Verderers' Court, which administers Forest laws, meets at Queen's House five times a year, but traffic routed on a lengthy one-way system round the town swishes past endlessly, blind to the beauty of seventeenth-century brick.

Outside the New Forest area, and the huge urban arc which rings Southampton and Portsmouth, Hampshire has some really fine small towns. At Alton, where traffic and modern frontages have largely destroyed a once-splendid street, occasional eighteenth-century houses have survived under commercial undertakings. Nevertheless, away from it, especially in Church Street, a quieter atmosphere prevails, while at the southern end of Alton the broad green space of The Butts preserves in its name a nice touch of the past, and round its edges some good groups of houses.

Botley and Wickham are small towns rather than large villages, and though markedly different in lay-out, both show small-scale townscapes to a high degree, each having sufficient numbers of well-placed larger buildings, eighteenth-century inns and houses, to add visual contrast and create an urban impression. Botley's High Street starts wide at the east, narrowing and curving towards the west out of sight. Wickham's pride is its enormous rectangular square, showing better than almost any other scene in Hampshire the priceless asset a large open space is, and how varied roof-lines, and occasional larger houses, emphasize visual delight in irregularity. There is nothing pretentious, out-of-scale, or brash – a bit of timber-framing, plenty of nice early Georgian, a touch or two of Victorian Gothic at the north, all mainly in grey and red brick, to make Wickham as good a place as you would want.

Petersfield gained its market charter in the twelfth century, prospered during the Middle Ages on wool, and then declined

Lyndhurst, Hampshire: the seventeenth-century Queen's House where the ancient Verderers' Court of the New Forest meets five times a year to administer Forest laws.

during the seventeenth century. Its position on the main London–Portsmouth road helped to revitalize the town from turnpike days onwards with two dozen coaches a day passing through, and now it still shows a Georgian affluence around the romanized statue of William III in the market place. Through traffic misses most of the town, leaving it to enjoy its marketing importance at the centre of a lush agricultural area.

Although Fareham is depressingly urbanized, with housing estates, supermarkets, window-stickers, chain stores and a multi-storey car park, its High Street makes up for a lot. Running north-wards at right angles to Fareham's main thoroughfare, East and West Street, to which trade has moved, High Street has kept com-merce and classical buildings. From its wider southern end, where the market-place has been partially built over, High Street narrows towards the north, with some particularly fine buildings on the eastern side.

My own favourites among Hampshire's small towns are New Alresford and Odiham. In 1200, the Bishop of Winchester cana-lized the River Alre, creating a huge pool to keep it supplied with water. From Old Alresford, a road follows the medieval dam along the western edge of this pool, now shrunk to a fraction of its former size, to the planted town of New Alresford on rising ground to the south. The market-place, laid out at right angles to the London road, is now Broad Street, still busy on Thursdays, when stalls front the elegant houses, many of them now shop-fronted, but not badly so. Towards the northern end trees provide their own contrast, making this one of Hampshire's most civilized streets, designed for people, used by people, and cared for by people.

So, obviously, is Odiham's High Street, although it suffers from too much traffic, especially 'heavies', thundering through to Aldershot. Nevertheless, it is a gem of a street, best appreciated by walking the whole length, down one side and back the other, with or without your Pevsner. Your own eye will recognize eight-eenth-century elegance, some nineteenth-century fronts, fine brickwork, and that oh-so-gentle curve at the east which contains the whole perspective. Odiham has a few oddities, such as the whipping-post and stocks, by the church, a Pest House on the southern edge of the churchyard, and, to the north-west of the town, by the Basingstoke Canal, the only octagonal castle keep in England, a flinty survivor of Odiham's castle of 1207.

Such places as these retain the country town flavour of Wessex, even if they are rather peripheral. Others have been less fortunate. Yeovil, almost in Sherborne's pocket, has no character whatsoever; to the north, Bruton's monastic glory has gone, and the town seems to live only through its famous schools and very beautiful church, having otherwise an atmosphere of faded gentility. Frome and Shepton Mallet have lost too much to developers, but local amenity societies have fought long, hard battles to save, here and there, little streets of human scale, oases of heritage. Glastonbury has lost even those. The greatest and holiest English shrine is a fragmented yet impressive ruin; in the town the George and Pilgrims' Inn, and the Abbot's Tribunal nearby, reach their historic hands through the centuries, but doubtless wring them in shame for what this century has done to Glastonbury – and continues to do. St Michael's Chapel, atop the Tor, echoes to the sound of transistors, canned music from ice-cream vans drifts upwards from Avalon, and nobody seems to care. At nearby Wells, the loveliest small cathedral city in England, litter floats plastically in the moat around the Bishop's Palace, but at least the priceless Cathedral Close preserves a quiet sanctity, and traffic is wisely kept at bay. The medieval market place has some good buildings, especially the old gateways between town and cathedral precinct. Yet I still think the best of Wells is the view you see from the eastern approach, a perfect little townscape skyline of towers and roofs against the Mendip background, enchantment at a distance.

What is the view of Wessex in the larger towns? As usual, the bigger they are, the more impersonal and remote they become, and the more scope for damage. Bath is the supreme example. True, the Georgian showpieces of one of Europe's finest cities are still there, The Royal Crescent, the Circus, Gay Street, Trim Street, Queen Square, and a number of smaller crescents, but huge chunks of the centre have been removed. Replacing them are examples of 1970 building incredible in their ugliness, violent in their crass disregard of neighbouring buildings and setting.

Intimate little streets for people, such as Northumberland Passage and Abbey Green, are delightful, a startling contrast to the newly pedestrianized precinct at the bottom of the town. The cuboid, angular Beaufort Hotel is now a backcloth to graceful Pulteney Bridge, while on all the surrounding hills, blocks replace

Above: *Bath Street, part of Baldwin's Bath Improvement Scheme of
1789. The fountain was erected in 1859.*

Opposite: *The Roman baths are twenty feet below the present street
levels. Layers of settlement shown here span nearly fifteen hundred years,
overlooked by the beautiful tower of Bath Abbey, near the former centre of
the Roman town.*

gentle curves. However, national horror, and a strong Preservation Trust, managed by 1973 to restrain further progress in the rape of Bath, and both government and the Trust are associated with the local authority to plan a more rational future for the city, which now houses, in addition to the Ministry of Defence, one of the major universities of modern Britain. Architecturally, culturally and in terms of its historic and literary associations, Bath is still the most outstanding place in Wessex. Its hot mineral springs made it famous, but now, a government decision has closed them down for treatment purposes, on the grounds of economy! One more administrative folly to add to that long list which has done so much to shred Bath's unique heritage.

Salisbury is only half the size of Bath, and there an emasculated conservation has come too late. Constable's famous view across the water-meadows is still astonishingly intact; the cathedral close is still all that such a place should be – grass, trees, good houses and relative peacefulness. It can never be completely quiet because of traffic noises in the streets nearby, and aircraft noises overhead, for Salisbury is surrounded by military establishments, as well as being the shopping and trading centre for a huge surrounding area, from the edge of the New Forest to beyond the Dorset boundary. When rainy days gloom southern beaches, summer holiday visitors forsake the coast for culture and history, finding both in Salisbury.

The market square is only a fraction of its original size. Adjacent streets like Ox Row and Fish Row were early encroachments on it, and today have some of the city's oldest houses. Poultry Cross is the only survivor of four medieval crosses, surrounded by chain stores and traffic, half-timbering and glass and concrete, and on Tuesdays and Saturdays the stalls of itinerant traders. The city used to be a great marketing centre for the huge amounts of wool produced on the vast sheep-walks of the Plain. Subsequently it turned to wool manufacture, sending finished cloth through Southampton to the continent. Surviving fifteenth- and sixteenth-century buildings were originally rich merchants' houses – John Halle's House (now part of a cinema!), John a'Port's House;

Salisbury Cathedral from the River Nadder, Wiltshire.

Salisbury Cathedral.

Winchester Cathedral (west front).

three inns also date from that time, The Haunch of Venison, The King's Arms, and The Old George, as well as two guildhalls. Medieval gateways, half-timbered houses, part of the original street plan, the Chequers, also contribute facets of the past, while other fragments hide behind modern frontages. A castrated type of conservation may be better than none at all, and modern ring-roads have certainly eased some traffic problems, but as so often is the case, city centre development, commercial and shopping, inevitably attracts more traffic to an already crowded area. More parking facilities are needed, and the multi-storey car parks add their own concrete misery.

Winchester is smaller than Salisbury, and so very much more rewarding for a seeker after Wessex. Its long status as capital has given it a proud security and its superb Norman cathedral has bestowed a benediction. During the Middle Ages it became an important centre for the wool trade, with easy access to the south coast bringing foreign merchants to the city for the annual St Giles' Fair, one of England's four great medieval fairs. William II had granted a charter for this to the bishops of Winchester, and during the sixteen days the fair lasted all shops within a radius of twenty miles had to close. The bishops benefited from this yearly medieval monopoly, the money went towards improving the cathedral, but the townsfolk did not like it.

By Tudor times the wool trade decreased, so that Elizabeth I's charter described Winchester as having fallen into decay, ruin and poverty. Fortunately it survived to become one of our most delightful small cathedral cities. Many medieval buildings remain, including two of the six original gateways, one with a tiny church on it. Near Westgate is the Plague Monument, where country folk deposited goods for the city, and townsfolk left money on a bowl of vinegar. To the south the Great Hall of the castle, built in 1235, is England's finest provincial medieval hall, and contains a remarkable piece of thirteenth-century furniture, an 18-foot-diameter table, designed to commemorate King Arthur, and painted in Tudor times. In the same Hall, Raleigh was sentenced to death in 1603, and Judge Jeffreys held court in 1685. Cromwell destroyed most of the castle, but the surrounding site is largely occupied by the late- and post-Victorian County Hall and its more modern appurtenances, representing a subtle continuity of power and authority.

Winchester is more intimate than Salisbury, its cathedral close more a part of human life, as are the famous College, founded by Bishop William of Wykeham in 1382, and St Cross Hospital, founded in 1133, with an added foundation of 1455. Crown, gown and town have continually contributed to Winchester's story, and their influence has been very strong. Each represents a human element, from the days of Alfred, whose modern statue looks towards High Street, Winchester's spine, and now partly traffic-free, down to the present, when as an honest traveller you may claim the Wayfarer's Dole at St Cross Hospital, and receive bread and ale. Beyond the city are the gently wooded hills of Hampshire, sliced through by new bypasses, and to the south the River Itchen flows serenely past St Catherine's Hill on its journey to the sea.

CHAPTER 4

VALES AND VILLAGES

ALTHOUGH SO MUCH of Wessex is chalk downland, most villages
are to be found along the valleys. By Anglo-Saxon times these had
become more accessible, with plenty of timber for building, and
water supply from chalk streams or springs emerging from the foot
of downland escarpments. Thus, strings of settlements are dispersed along the valleys radiating from Salisbury Plain, and the
downs of Berkshire, Hampshire and Dorset. On the rich soils in
these vales villages could be built quite close together, since they
had the further advantage of upland grazings of the land on each
side of the vales. By travelling along these vales you can obtain,
not one view but a series of views of Wessex villages, and since the
'feel' of Wessex tends to strengthen the further west you go, I propose to start in the east and north, gradually working my way
towards Dorchester and the heart of Hardy's Wessex.

The steep scarp face of the North Wessex Downs is the northern
frontier of our Wessex, and looks across the Vale of the White
Horse. From Wantage eastwards to Streatley the A417 keeps close
to the spring-line, while westwards to Swindon the B4507 continues the process, linking more than twenty villages in a distance
of thirty-three miles. Aston Tirrold, Aston Upthorpe, Upton,
Blewbury, the Hagbournes and the Hendreds manage to keep

Eighteenth-century cottages in the Estate Village at Stourton.

Didcot's ulcerous spread at bay, but only just, and Harwell is far too close for comfort, but cottages of brick and timber, some with thatch, preserve a degree of character in most of these villages. Further to the west, timber is used less, and sarsen stones from the downs find their way into a number of villages, particularly Ashbury and Bishopstone, making you realize what an unusually attractive building stone it is.

To the south the Vale of Lambourn makes a shallow trough in the rolling downland landscape. More famous as a centre for training thoroughbred racehorses than as Hardy's Maryland in *Jude the Obscure*, Lambourn is a large, attractive village below which its river flows south-east, clear and many-pooled, by East Garston, Great Shelford, Welford and Boxford to join the Kennet at Newbury. This chalk stream has very sketchy beginnings on the downs near Avebury, and does not merit a name on the Ordnance Survey map until it almost reaches Marlborough. Nevertheless, few English rivers are baptized so historically, trickling as it does by Avebury's great circle and Silbury's enigmatic mound. A4 travellers catch occasional glimpses of it, except in dry seasons, between West Kennet and Marlborough, but east of the town the river follows a northerly loop to Hungerford, through Mildenhall and Ramsbury.

Mildenhall's perfect village church adds distinction to the Vale of Kennet, revealing many periods from Anglo-Saxon onwards, and a completely unspoilt interior surviving from its refurnishing of 1815–16. Ramsbury was the site of a Saxon bishopric, and very recently this See has been revived. Very much a 'street' village it has many good houses of the seventeenth and eighteenth centuries, and Ramsbury Manor to the west, unfortunately not easy to see from the road nor open to the public, is a perfect example of a brick mansion of 1680, designed by Inigo Jones's son-in-law, John Webb. Littlecote House, lower down the Kennet, is open to view, also brick-built, mainly Elizabethan but with some parts obviously older, although the chapel is of Cromwell's time. The Darell family who lived at Littlecote gained some notoriety in the sixteenth century through the reckless exploits of 'Wild Darell', who seems to have escaped the law, possibly because a relative, Sir John

Sarsen stones and a cottage made from them, at Lockeridge Dene in the Kennet valley, near Marlborough, Wiltshire.

Popham, was Attorney General.

At Hungerford the A4 rejoins the Kennet valley, as does the Kennet and Avon Canal, the three continuing in close company eastwards to Newbury. Hungerford has fishing rights in the river, granted in the fourteenth century by John of Gaunt, who also gave the town a horn. This is used each year on the Tuesday after Easter as part of the Hocktide ceremony associated with these ancient rights when two tutti-men (tithe-collectors) carrying a pole decorated with flowers go round claiming kisses from pretty girls. For the rest of the year Hungerford remains a pleasant market town with a broad High Street, good coaching inns, a lack of industrialization and a splendid stretch of open and wooded common land to the south-east.

Newbury is gnawing away its surrounding countryside, and villages within its commuting territory suffer accordingly.

To the south of the town the River Enborne marks Berkshire's boundary with Hampshire, with the A34 and A343 cutting southwards through wooded countryside to Winchester and Andover respectively. Between them is Highclere Castle, Hampshire's largest house, a rebuilding by Sir Charles Barry for the third Earl of Caernarvon, 1839–42. The earlier house was a classical eighteenth-century design, far more appropriate to Capability Brown's beautifully landscaped park of 1774–7 than the present Gothic and turreted structure. Two miles away, at Burghclere, is something very different, the Sandham Memorial Chapel, commemorating a Lieutenant H. W. Sandham who died in 1919. Mr and Mrs J. L. Behrend commissioned Stanley Spencer to paint the inside, using a cycle of war-paintings he was working on, and the result is the finest English monument to twentieth-century Expressionism, embodied in nineteen huge, awe-inspiring and movingly beautiful paintings carried out between 1927 and 1932. The National Trust own the Chapel, so that the public can see Spencer's genius expressed in the muted greys, browns and greens, sad undertones of the boredom of war.

North-east Hampshire was a densely wooded area in medieval days and the easy availability and cheapness of wood made it the obvious building material, not only for houses and barns but for churches as well. A few of these can still be seen to the north of Odiham, where the church at Mattingley is timber-framed throughout, and the fifteenth-century tower of Yateley's church has north, south and west aisles similar to those in half-timbered bell-towers of some East Anglian churches. But for unique bold fantasy Hartley Wespall stands supreme, having in its west wall an extraordinary framework, cusped-lozenge shaped, repeated at smaller scale in the gable, the only part of the fourteenth-century building to survive.

In delightful contrast, and only a few miles to the west, is one of Hampshire's finest houses. The Vyne, now owned by the National Trust, was built by Lord Sandys, Henry VIII's Lord Chancellor, between 1518 and 1527, extensively altered in 1655, and again in the 1760s by John Chute. The Classical north portico of 1655 by John Webb is the earliest domestic one in England, built of brick

The River Test near Stockbridge, Hampshire.

and having a wooden pediment, part of a most beautiful and stately north front mirrored in the lake.

Hampshire's main rivers, Test, Itchen and Meon, flow southwards to the Solent, carrying in their clear waters a memory of the chalk and a piscator's pleasure. The countryside of their valleys, and of the chalklands which give them birth, is probably not greatly changed from the days when Jane Austen and Gilbert White were living in eastern Hampshire. Chawton, a village on the outskirts of Alton, was the novelist's home from 1809 to 1817. At Chawton Cottage (open to the public) she revised *Sense and Sensibility* and wrote *Mansfield Park*, *Emma* and *Persuasion*, and from there saw four of her books published. Nearby are numerous spring-fed streams which merge into the River Wey, and flow north and north-west into Surrey.

A few miles down the B3006 is Selborne, birthplace and home of Gilbert White, 1720–93. Born at the Vicarage, he spent most of his life in and around the area, being curate at Selborne from the 1750s. Usually regarded primarily as a naturalist, it is as well to remember that he was an antiquarian too, as the full title of his book indicates. He was an original observer and an out-standingly skilful writer, a man concerned with the total story of his environment. His greatest contribution to Wessex and to England was not so much his book but the fact that it was the forerunner of hundreds of examples of observant and tender care lavished on other villages and parishes, leading to an increased awareness and curiosity about the environment. His house, The Wakes, is a memorial library and museum to himself and Captain Oates, but White's spirit is in the beech-hangers around the village, on Selborne Common and in the leafy lanes and field paths.

The Meon is only twenty miles long, a good length for a river, just enough to give it character and yet still allow it to be explored, by car at least, in a day. Quiet lanes lead to it from the enfolding downs, and near the river's head East Meon is one of Hampshire's best villages, full of good houses especially in the High Street, half-timber and thatch nicely mixed in with Georgian symmetry, along the side of a stream. Court House is medieval, the church opposite magnificent, with one of the four Tournai black marble fonts in the county, a vigorous creation of about 1130. At West Meon a few miles away the A32 comes down the valley, shattering some of its peacefulness without actually destroying villages like Warnford and Droxford.

Hambledon is a T-shaped village with plenty of timber-framed and Georgian houses, in some of which, no doubt, members of the famous Hambledon cricket team would have lived in the eighteenth century. They played on Broadhalfpenny Down two miles away, the great years being from 1772 to 1790, Hampshire v. All England at £500 a side. From these early beginnings the rules of the game evolved, the MCC was founded, and cricket enriched the English-speaking world.

East Meon, Hampshire, from Park Hill.

Meon valley, Hampshire, from West Meon.

Titchfield Abbey, Hampshire, was converted in 1542 by the Earl of Southampton into a fine Tudor mansion, called Place House, of which this spectacular gatehouse survives.

In a paddock at Hambledon Major-General Sir Guy Salisbury-Jones planted a few vines in 1952, almost as an amusing hobby for his retirement. The vineyard has trebled in size to 4½ acres and now produces nearly 4,000 bottles of white wine annually, of outstandingly good quality. There are occasional open days during late summer and early autumn when the vineyard can be visited.

Wickham has already been mentioned, and by way of adding a final benediction to the river, the gatehouse of Titchfield Abbey is a monastic remnant. Across the A27 Titchfield itself is more a small town than a large village, with a number of delightful houses, mainly Georgian brick, and some with Dutch roof tiles, a reminder that it was once a seaport trading with the Low Countries. The estuary was drained in the seventeenth century, and a wall built across the river. Although a canal was cut, Titchfield lost its importance to Fareham, and seems to have escaped the worse excesses of the nineteenth and twentieth centuries, a remarkable achievement for a place midway between Portsmouth and Southampton. How long it can hold out remains to be seen, for subtopia is lurking in the wings.

A small chalk stream flows southwards from the surviving woodlands of Micheldever Forest, to join the River Itchen west of Alresford. It passes the Candover villages, Preston, Chilton and Brown, the first being the largest with attractive cottage groups, and the second having a ruined church with a Norman crypt revealed in 1925. Lower down its course the stream widens into a lake in the parklands of The Grange at Northington, a monumental piece of architecture remodelled by Wilkins in 1804–9, with an enormous Parthenon portico desertedly dominating the quietly controlled landscape. A few miles south, beyond the A31, the infant Itchen wanders through water-meadows from Cheriton, a straggly village, and Tichborne, a thatched one, whose lovely church has a late Saxon chancel and a 1700 tower of red and blue bricks. The Tichborne family are still at Tichborne House, having lived there since before the Conquest. They initiated the Tichborne Dole in 1150, when Sir Roger agreed to his wife's request for a village dole based on land to support the charity.

The Itchen is better above Winchester than below, the villages more worthy of their setting; literally so, since four of them have it in their name, Martyr, Abbots, King's and Headbourne Worthy which with Itchen Stoke and Itchen Abbas are on the north side of the valley. But Avington, opposite Itchen Abbas has compensation in its superb little brick church of 1768 retaining original wood-work and furnishings, and some fine monuments.

The Test is one of England's great trout rivers, flowing for most of its course through a broad green valley, with reeds and water-meadows peacefully fringing its fishermen-frequented banks. Rising in the chalky uplands west of Basingstoke it becomes, past Whitchurch, two streams and is joined by the Bourne Rivulet coming down from Hurstbourne Tarrant and St Mary Bourne, with its watercress beds to Hurstbourne Priors. At Laverstoke, Henri Portal, a Huguenot refugee, having made the first water-marked paper in 1712, built a mill, where since 1724 Bank of England notes have been made. High walls surround the newer buildings, and Laverstoke House nearby was built in 1796 for Harry Portal. Another tributary flows in from the east, to the ac-companiment of euphonic double-barrelled place-names, Michel-dever, Weston Colley, Stoke Charity, Sutton Scotney and Barton Stacey, from each of which straight enclosure roads lead to the beech-clumped downs. Bullington has a group of buildings beautifully placed by the stream, church, barn and Tudor house, but in the main valley Wherwell and Longstock can claim to be a pair of Hampshire's prettiest villages. The twin-channel Test here has on its banks circular thatched huts used by anglers, and at Leck-ford is an important trout hatchery.

Stockbridge looks like a town, but its main street running east–west has hardly any lanes behind it. Most of its buildings are early nineteenth century, colourful, with varied roof lines, while the two main hotels, Grosvenor and White Hart, one with a huge overhanging porch on new columns, the other whose whole front stands on cast-iron columns, are headquarters of visiting anglers. Stockbridge's claim to notoriety is that it was regarded as the most corrupt of all the rotten boroughs, before the Reform Bill of 1832, exemplified by Sir Richard Steele, who, when canvassing support, is said to have promised an apple stuffed with guineas to the first couple to have a child after his election. Unfortunately for them, he was not elected.

King's Somborne and Mottisfont are the main villages between Stockbridge and Romsey. Mottisfont Abbey, surrounded by wide lawns, beech, chestnuts and cedars, was really only a small priory which after the Dissolution passed into the hands of Lord Sandys, of The Vyne, who lived in the nave of the priory church. Extensive remodelling took place about 1740, the date of the present brick house facing south, which came into National Trust keeping in 1957. Below Romsey the Test contains salmon but begins to lose its essentially rural character as it approaches the tidal reaches at the head of Southampton Water.

Back in the northern part of Wessex, the River Avon, born among the southern slopes of the Cotswolds, and gradually developing into a clay vale river before a final dramatic exit to the Bristol Channel, is very much more a river of industry. Its circuitous course starts in the great park at Badminton, takes it north-east through Luckington and Sherston to Malmesbury, and southwards by the Somerfords to Chippenham. Within this large loop are three of England's loveliest villages, Castle Combe, Biddestone and Sherston itself, each typifying a particular village shape. Castle Combe is grouped round the nucleus of its small triangular market place. Biddestone spreads itself around an elongated green with a fine pond at one end, and Sherston has one very wide street, and a parallel but narrower one to the west. Each has fine houses of the seventeenth and eighteenth centuries, the Georgian ones representing the prosperity of wool merchants.

Aldhelm knew the Avon at Malmesbury; Princess Anne knows it at Great Somerford, where her husband Captain Mark Phillips lived at the delightful old manor-house. Nearer Chippenham the wide flood plain of the river was a medieval hazard to travellers, so a market woman, Maud Heath, built a causeway in the fifteenth century, and the main-line expresses roar past, nearby, on Brunel's great line from London to Bristol. Nearer Chippenham the line goes through Box Tunnel, which took five years to build and has boldly Classical portals at each end.

South of Chippenham, the Avon touches Lacock, yet another

Above: *A moated manor-house – Great Chalfield near Bradford-on-Avon, seen from the south.*

Opposite: *One of the most famous sites of Cerne Abbas, Dorset – "The Pitchmarket" in historic Abbey Street.*

fine village, which, with its sixteenth-century abbey converted from a former nunnery, and changed again in the eighteenth century, is all National Trust property. Together with Kodak Ltd, the Trust has restored a magnificent barn to house the Fox-Talbot collection of photographs and apparatus associated with this inventive, scientific, philosophical, early Victorian squire of Lacock, one of the pioneers of photography. The Avon becomes more industrial from Melksham onwards, although it flows through very pleasant farming country to Bradford-on-Avon. There, it enters a narrower wooded valley, part of which is a new Country Park designated by Wiltshire County Council, and based on the medieval Barton Farm and famous tithe barn. For the rest of its way to Bath, the river, Kennet and Avon Canal and railway move in close company. At Freshford the River Frome joins the Avon, bringing with it a memory of mills and small wool villages, of stone bridges and merchants' houses, of Lullington, Orchardleigh, Beckington, Rode, Tellisford, Farleigh and Iford, while the larger and more famous Norton St Philip is only a couple of miles away. For domestic building, for small country houses from the fifteenth to eighteenth centuries, and for villages remarkably little spoilt, this part of the Avon valley is as good as anywhere in Wessex. On either side of its valley between Bradford and Bath the limestone hills have been mined for stone. Mined, not quarried, for the best strata are several feet beneath the surface. At Westwood and Limpley Stoke, but more especially between Bathford and Corsham, underground galleries stretch for great distances, and in the area around Box there are sixty miles of such workings, many of which belong to the Ministry of Defence, and only that at Monk's Park is still being worked. A few of the now disused ones, perhaps above Bathford, should be made into the nucleus of a unique stone-mining industrial museum before they deteriorate further. There is nothing like them in Britain, and they could be an additional tourist attraction, near Bath, and almost in view of the well-known American Museum at Claverton Manor.

In central Wiltshire the Vale of Pewsey extends as a broad swathe eastwards from Devizes to Savernake Forest, five miles wide with no river to speak of, between Salisbury Plain on the

Great Chalfield Manor, near Bradford-on-Avon, Wiltshire, was built (1470–80) by a great clothier, Thomas Tropenell, and is one of the finest of Britain's late medieval manor-houses.

south and the Marlborough Downs on the north, the highest continuous chalk wall in Wessex with three summits above 900 feet. Roads along each side of the vale link a series of villages, none spectacular, all with pleasant black-and-white half-timbering, and most farms have both clay land and chalk down, making them some of the best in Wessex. Cobbett was most impressed during his stay at Milton Lilbourne in 1826, and wrote that "it would be impossible to find a more beautiful and pleasant country than this". Ever practical, he calculated that the wheat, barley, wool, pigs and poultry in one parish could provide bread for 800 families, mutton for 500, and bacon and beer for over 200.

Near Devizes, Bishop's Cannings claims immortality as the source of the Moonrakers. Two local men were seen one moonlit night raking a pond's surface with hay rakes, explaining when asked, and pointing to the moon's reflection in the water, that they were trying to retrieve that big round cheese. Their challengers rode away laughing at such apparent simple-wittedness. As they were excisemen seeking smugglers, the locals had the last laugh, knowing there were kegs of brandy hidden in the pond for safety. Local gossips quickly circulated the tale, and folklore soon versified it. Now Wiltshiremen are 'Moonrakers' and proud of it. Pewsey, at the other end of the vale, is a large village, or small town, with one of Wessex's King Alfred statues, and good wharfside buildings by the Kennet and Avon Canal which windingly threads its way in a single pound along the vale.

Pewsey Vale has over two dozen villages in its twelve mile length, emphasizing the land's fertility. Although it is really an extension eastwards of the Bristol Avon, the river which is eventually formed out of the streams merging south of Pewsey is the Salisbury Avon, which flows curvingly through a gap in the chalk at Upavon, forming a narrow valley with downlands rising steeply on each side. Small villages mark its course to Amesbury, but with Tidworth and Bulford Camps on its eastern margin, Larkhill to the west, and an important airfield at Upavon, the military presence is emphatically marked.

Below Amesbury the Avon is more wooded and rural, with good houses of brick and flint. Narrowing tongues of chalk downland separate it from other rivers converging on Salisbury, Bourne to the east, Wylye and Nadder to the west, whose wider valleys are scenically much more pleasant to explore. The River Wylye started life as the Deverill close to the Somerset border, almost within roaring distance of the lions of Longleat. The great house itself occupies the site of a medieval priory which, after the Dissolution, was bought by Sir John Thynne. After fire destroyed it in 1567 he set about building the fine mansion we see today, the first of the "Elizabethan prodigy houses" as Sir John Summerson

Wilton Mill in the Vale of Pewsey, Wiltshire. 147

Above: *A man-made landscape – looking north-west from Swallowcliffe Down, south Wiltshire.*

Opposite: *Longcombe Bottom and Blackmore Vale, Dorset, with the slopes of Fontmell Down on the right.*

Fonthill Gifford, Wiltshire: the gatehouse to the Fonthill Estate, possibly built from a design by Inigo Jones, c.1635.

describes them. Building started about 1572, but Thynne died before it was completed. Longleat has no 'back', but four symmetrical façades, and internally there was a big reconstruction in the early 1800s. Capability Brown remodelled the park about 1760, and Repton worked there thirty years later, but the biggest change came in the 1960s when the present Marquess of Bath pioneered the idea of introducing wild animals to an inner section of the park. With the help of Jimmy Chipperfield, the scheme was successfully carried out, and by now millions of visitors must have seen the lions of Longleat, with the many other species which have been introduced from foreign lands into this most English of Wessex countrysides. But I still think the view of Longleat from the woods by Heaven's Gate far better than the close inspection; the picture is in its frame.

To the south and east the Deverill valley runs between rounded chalk shoulders, becoming the Wylye near Warminster, flowing as a clear chalk stream past a succession of villages of brick and flint, stone and thatch. With the main A36 on the north, villages on the southern side of the Wylye are quieter and generally prettier, with Stockton and Sherrington taking the honours. Near Great Wishford the tiny River Till joins the Wylye, having originated on the heart of Salisbury Plain to the north, where Tilshead was a prosperous town at the time of Domesday, one of the largest in Wiltshire, presumably because of the existence of large-scale sheep farming on the Plain. As far as Shrewton the Till is more often dry than not, but in 1841 it became a raging torrent many feet deep, just before nightfall, and swept away many cottages in villages along its path. The old stone lock-up at Shrewton survived, but very recently has been dismantled and re-erected near its former site, in a position less vulnerable to damage by heavy lorries and army vehicles.

The River Nadder rises close to the foot of the downs near Shaftesbury, and flows north-east through the Donheads to Tisbury. To the north the woods of Fonthill recall the great eccentric William Beckford, eighteenth-century millionaire son of a Lord Mayor of London. Between 1796 and 1812 he built England's most monumental Gothic folly, employing up to 500 workmen at a time. A central tower was 225 feet high in the middle of a cathedral-like building 350 feet long. Around his estate he constructed a 12-foot wall, much of which still stands, but Fonthill Abbey collapsed in 1825, two years after Beckford had moved out to live at Bath. It really had been jerry-built.

At Chilmark, and to a lesser degree at Tisbury, a fine-grained creamy-coloured limestone has been quarried from medieval times until 1937, and used in many famous buildings, Salisbury Cathedral, Romsey Abbey, Wilton House, Longford Castle, Wardour Castle, and fine houses and cottages in villages along the valley of the Nadder, making this part of Wessex particularly rewarding architecturally. As well as Chilmark itself, all the villages are attractive, Hindon, the Teffonts, Dinton, Baverstock and Barford on the north side, Ansty, Swallowcliffe, Sutton Mandeville, Fovant and Compton Chamberlayne on the south, each of these lying just off the A30 trunk road to Exeter, and very thankful to be so. The road along the north of the Nadder valley eventually reaches East Knoyle, sitting snugly at the foot of a 'hanger' type of downland slope. Here was born Sir Christopher Wren, son of the seventeenth-century rector, and perhaps as a youngster he may have absorbed something of the splendour of local stone, although it was to the whiter limestone of Portland that he turned for his London churches.

The old road from Salisbury to Shaftesbury followed the crest of the downs south of the Nadder, and still has one or two eighteenth-century milestones placed there by the Earl of Pembroke, rather more permanent than the mile trees he also planted, but which have now gone, together with the refreshment places, at Fovant and Compton Huts. Beyond the ridge the land slopes more gently to the Ebble valley, secretive, shy and not afflicted with a busy road. Villages muse quietly away by the tiny stream which lower down its course idles through watercress beds. Berwick St John, Alvediston, Ebbesbourne Wake, Combe Bisset and Odstock mark off its gentle progress through sixteen sleepy miles. Busy men have chosen to live by its meadows, Sir Cecil Beaton, Lord Avon and the detective novelist John Creasey, while Donhead St Mary, to the west, was for a time the home of historian Sir Arthur Bryant.

The Ebble joins the Avon near Longford Castle, home of the Earls of Radnor since 1717, a country house which looks like a castle, its eastern walls washed by the Avon's tranquil waters, in a setting of lawns, formal gardens and woodlands. Designed about 1580 as the first triangular Elizabethan mansion, with towers at the corners, it was extensively rebuilt by Salvin in the 1870s as near the original as possible. Across the river Alderbury's inn The Green Dragon has changed its colour from The Blue Dragon in *Martin Chuzzlewit*, Dickens having stayed there while gathering material for his book. A few miles away, Downton marks the end of Wiltshire. The village has its main street at right angles to the Salisbury–Bournemouth road, the Anglo-Saxon settlement being on the east bank of the river around the site of the parish church, but in the twelfth century a bishop of Winchester planted a new town to the west of the river, where the main road now carries

Breamore Church in the Avon valley, Wiltshire.

busy traffic to and from the south coast. On the down to the
west, among woodlands and plantations, is an ancient Mizmaze
cut in the turf.

By now the Avon is not one stream but many and increasing
areas of woodland signify its entering the New Forest. Half-
timbering becomes more common, both at Breamore and Wood
Green. Breamore House has been owned only by two families
since it was built in 1583, but reconstruction after a fire in 1856
has changed some of its Tudor character. The stables house a car-
riage museum, while in the grounds is the Breamore Countryside
Museum, with a fine collection of agricultural implements and
machinery, together with reconstructions of a dairy, a black-
smith's, a wheelwright's and a farm brewery, illustrating old
crafts. Rockbourne, on the downs to the west, has a chalk stream
running down it, a vital element in one of Hampshire's most attractive street villages, with timber-framed thatched houses. An

153

impressively large Roman villa was discovered in 1942 on the site of the village cricket field, and summer excavations each year since 1956 have revealed a complex estate mansion of over seventy rooms, with many mosaic pavements and some baths.

Below Fordingbridge the Avon loops and curves its meadowly way, passing very few villages, but through an increasingly heathy, wooded, and subsequently suburbanized countryside to Ringwood and the edges of the Bournemouth sprawl. It finally enters the sea at the head of Christchurch Harbour, close to the mouth of the River Stour, whose meandering course has brought it from the western edge of Salisbury Plain through eastern Dorset.

The Stour is emphatically a river of Wessex, so it is appropriate that its source should be in an area closely linked with Alfred. Stourhead is not so called without good reason, and I like to think that in a beautiful hollow grove not far from Alfred's Tower the Stour emerges as a tiny spring. Around are planted woodlands of what many regard as the most beautiful manmade landscape in England. About 1741 Henry Hoare, a member of the banking family, dammed the infant Stour to create a large lake, added a series of Classical and Gothic buildings, Pantheon, Temple of Flora, bridge, rustic cottage, obelisk, statues and grotto, all within the next twenty years, then shifted more earth, planted trees, and contrived with immense skill and sense to produce an idealized nature mainly for the benefit of future generations. In Victorian times a later Hoare planted the many exotic shrubs, but Stourhead House itself is the almost pure Palladian design of Colen Campbell's in 1721–24, wings being added at the end of the century. Happily, both house and grounds are in the safe hands of the National Trust.

A few miles away Mere, now bypassed by the A303, is Wiltshire's western outpost of the chalk, its name an old word meaning 'boundary'. Good houses and inns, The Ship proudly displaying a beautiful wrought-iron sign, and a handsome church, give Mere the appearance of a small town rather than a village, and the view from Castle Hill shows serrated downland edges to the north, Stourhead's woods to the west, and the broad, fertile fields and pastures of Blackmore Vale to the south. From Wincanton

Mere, Wiltshire, viewed from Castle Hill, looking towards Blackmore Vale.

comes the River Cale and from East Knoyle the River Lodden, to amalgamate with the Stour below Gillingham, and in this rich farming countryside villages are rarely more than three miles apart.

Its heavy clay soil, with many muddy streams, low hills and

undulations, made the vale poor for the pioneers of prehistoric times, but prosperous for farmers who came later. Sixty generations of husbandry have taken little account of conquerors and kings, plagues and pestilences. Hardy described his 'Vale of Little Dairies' as having "fields which are never brown and springs which are never dry". In many respects, Blackmore Vale and Dorset's other clay vale, Marshwood, have probably changed less than any other region in the county, although draining and re-seeding has probably added as much as six weeks to their growing season, giving increased milk yields from their dairy cattle. Fields are still small, lanes linking villages and wandering from one farm to another do so in a very haphazard way suggestive of possible prehistoric forest tracks, or of boundary hollow-ways originating in Saxon times.

There is no easy way of exploring Blackmore Vale. The A350 from Shaftesbury winds its way along the western foot of the scarp-edge of Cranborne Chase by Fontmell Magna and Iwerne Minster, while on the vale's western edge the A357 passes a number of small villages along its route from Wincanton to Blandford, with Stalbridge and Sturminster Newton the most important places. An elegant fifteenth-century market cross points to Stalbridge's earlier importance, and many of the farms to the south-east were first recorded in medieval times, as forest and wastes were being enclosed. Sturminster Newton was also an important market centre, where Thomas and Emma Hardy rented a Victorian villa on the edge of the town, overlooking the river, and where Hardy wrote *The Return of the Native* during the two happiest years of his life. The widely scattered village of Marnhull between Shaftesbury and Stalbridge was Tess's home in *Tess of the d'Urbervilles*, so in this part of Dorset I feel that Wessex landscape, literature, villages and people fuse together in a clearer view.

Blackmore Vale extends westwards almost to Yetminster and Ryme Intrinsica (echoes of Betjeman's lovely poem about Dorset's euphonic place-names), picking up the feeder streams of Cam and Caundle, with the A3030 giving main-road access. Neither Wessex in general nor Dorset in particular can really be explored thoroughly from main roads. You need Ordnance Survey Maps,

Hammoon Manor, Dorset.

preferably the new 1:50,000 series, to take you safely along the lanes and lead you to unexpected discoveries, splendid stone manor-houses, fine churches and old bridges, in an atmosphere of apparent timelessness.

Mappowder, Hammoon, Purse Caundle, Bingham's Melcombe and Fontleroi do not dominate but obviously belong to this gentle landscape, like the dialect poems of William Barnes. Feeder streams add their own quality to the Stour's maturing character. Near Blandford the Tarrant gives its name to eight settlements, but further east the River Allen makes no similar contribution to its villages, Wimborne St Giles (with its beautiful group of church and almshouses), the Gussages, Moor Crichel and Witchampton,

*Higher Bockhampton, near Dorchester: the cottage, c.1800, where
Thomas Hardy was born in 1841, and where he wrote some of his novels
and poems.*

while nearby are the fine house at Edmonsham behind its lovely
church, and the gaunt brick folly of Horton Tower crowning a
hilltop on the edge of heathy forest. At Wimborne the Stour fights
urban invasion of its secrecy and loses the contest.

Dorset's other main river, the Frome, starts its journey around
Evershot and the Melburys, Bubb, Osmond and Sampford, the
country of the Strangways, one of Dorset's great families. Sir Giles
was a commissioner for the surrender of Dorset monasteries, a
profitable post, for he built Melbury Sampford in 1540, acquired
most of the Abbotsbury Abbey lands the same year, as well as large
estates in Blackmore Vale and added a huge park to his own house,
while his successors in the family continued to add to the estates.
From the west, the tiny River Hooke brings a memory of the
lovely house at Mapperton and the remnants of Hooke Court
before joining the Frome at Maiden Newton, where river, road

and railway head eastwards to Dorchester. The River Cerne trickles its chalky way southwards from Minterne Magna, along a steep-sided valley, and the Winterbourne takes an easterly course south of Dorchester to join the Frome at West Stafford. Across the river is Stinsford, made up of three hamlets, four big houses, a number of farms, no inn and no shop other than the post office. As Hardy's Mellstock in *Under the Greenwood Tree* it was virtually the same, but now, in the tree-shaded churchyard, Cecil Day Lewis lies close to the heart of Thomas Hardy, and a school occupies Stinsford House.

On the edge of Puddletown Forest and Heath to the north-east is Higher Bockhampton, where Hardy was born in 1840, and later wrote his first, but unpublished, novel *The Poor Man and the Lady*, followed in 1871 by *Desperate Remedies* and *Under the Greenwood Tree*, and in 1874 *Far from the Madding Crowd*. Now owned by the National Trust, the outside of the cottage can be seen at any time, the inside by appointment with the tenant. If one building could be said to enshrine the heart of Wessex, this is it, yet there are scores of similar cottages throughout much of Dorset. Much of the land between here and Bournemouth is still heathy in character, though the Forestry Commission, the Army and expanding towns have made big inroads. Most of its isolated cottages which Hardy knew have gone, and the villages have become much smaller, in spite of many housing estates which fringe them.

No main road mars the Frome valley between Dorchester and Wool. The A352 keeps well to the south, by Broadmayne and Owermoigne, while the busier A35 cuts north-east to Puddletown, following the River Piddle for three miles before the river leaves for a slightly more southerly journey between Wareham Forest and Bovington Camp.

Puddletown was Weatherbury in *Far from the Madding Crowd*, and the inside of its church escaped the Victorians, remaining very much a period-piece of Jacobean woodwork and atmosphere. The best part of the village is north of the main road, with an attractive square fronted by colour-washed thatched cottages. A mile up the Piddle valley is Druce Farm (Squire Boldwood's home), and further on is Waterston Manor, an early Renaissance house, and

Bathsheba Everdine's home, though slightly modified after a disastrous fire in 1863. In reality it belonged to the Martyn family before they built the larger Athelhampton House between 1470 and 1490, which has a few later additions that do not mar the glorious lack of symmetry characteristic of such houses.

Tolpuddle looks better from the river valley than from the main road, and its TUC Cottages of 1933 are one of a number of local memorials to that famous band of agricultural labourers who illegally formed a union in 1833 to oppose a fall in their wages, and were subsequently sentenced to transportation to Australia for seven years, later reduced.

Bere Regis, the second part of whose name arises from medieval associations with Kings John, Henry III and Edward I, is a disappointing village. However, its church has the best timber roof in Dorset, hammer-beamed, with carved and gilded figures and bosses, a shining structure of fifteenth-century splendour. The heathy country through which the Piddle continues its course has no villages on it, and although the river approaches the Frome it never joins it. Wool is the main village between Dorchester and Wareham, but with military camps to the north and Winfrith Nuclear Research Station to the west, expansion is inevitably enveloping the older village. Woolbridge Manor, with its d'Urberville associations, fortunately remains isolated north of the river, a pleasant hotel in a seventeenth-century building.

Rivers of west Dorset are small, with short, significant lives and even shorter names, Bride, Brit, Simene and Char. The Bride's course by rounded chalk downs takes in Little Bredy, Long Bredy, the great mansion of Kingston Russell, and Litton Cheney before it meets the sea at Burton Bradstock. Beaminster blesses the birth of the Brit which takes an unusually direct route to the sea at West Bay, and the Simene and Char drain opposite ends of Marshwood Vale, ringed by steep green ramparts of hills, Lambert's Castle, Pilsdon Pen, Burstock Down, Waddon Hill and Coppet Hill. Steep-banked, high-hedged lanes thread the clayey bottom, and villages are dispersed round the edge, Whitchurch Canonicorum, Wootton Fitzpaine, Marshwood, Broadwindsor, Stoke Abbott, Symondsbury and Morecombelake.

Beyond the ridge of hills to the north the River Axe forms a Wessex frontier dignified by Forde Abbey, a Cistercian foundation of 1141, much rebuilt by its last abbot, Thomas Chard, just before the Dissolution. Edward Prideaux, Cromwell's Attorney General, bought it about 1650, and gave the south front a new centre, so that the building today represents one of the best examples of a medieval monastery incorporated into a sixteenth- and seventeenth-century country house.

The Foss Way forms a useful boundary to this view of western Wessex. To the north of Crewkerne it carries a main road to Bath, initially the A303, then A37, and beyond Shepton Mallet A367. Built by the Romans as a frontier route, it is today a main road to the West Country. Yet it retains, geographically at least, frontier characteristics, with undulating country to the east and lowland landscapes to the west. Within easy reach is the Tudor mansion of Montacute, the smaller houses at Lytes Cary and Tintinhull, all National Trust. From Ham Hill quarries came one of the loveliest of building stones, warm-toned and textured, which give to local houses and churches their unique golden sunlight glow. The Hamdons, East Coker, Martock, and Montacute show this to perfection, emphasizing how beautiful are some building stones in contrast to the mass-produced materials used in so many modern houses.

CHAPTER 5

ALONG THE COAST

WESSEX HAS NO COAST, or if it has you never hear about it. Other historic regions of England are more fortunate, both Northumbria and East Anglia having named and famous coastlines. But when it comes to the shores of the Channel Wessex loses its regional and historic identity in favour of its two counties which actually have a southern seaboard, Hampshire and Dorset. Since so much of the Hampshire coast has been swallowed up by the hungry spread of Portsmouth and Southampton, and the county has lost Christchurch and Bournemouth to Dorset anyway, there is nothing left of what the National Trust would call 'Heritage Coastline' in Hampshire. So the notion of a Wessex coast becomes in reality the Dorset coast. Nevertheless, since Hampshire is part of Wessex we must pay some attention to what there is of coastal character.

Portsmouth can reasonably claim to be the only British city on an island, Portsea Island, which is separated from the mainland by Port Creek, so that Portsmouth Harbour is to the west and Langstone Harbour to the east. Although two main roads and the railway cross this water by bridges, the new motorway approach has been constructed on a causeway, so that in the technical sense now, Portsea Island has become a peninsula. This motorway also makes

"The Dancing Ledges" near Langton Matravers, Dorset.

Portsmouth one of the easiest cities both to enter or to leave, by road. Indeed, road-signs in the centre of the city are the best I have encountered in Wessex, clearly pointing directions to the important parts, and for the departing travellers the explicit instruction 'Out of Town'. Not that you should be wanting to leave too soon, for Portsmouth, being what it is, deserves a prolonged stay and exploration.

Portchester, on the north side of the harbour, was a Roman fort, used later by the Normans, but as the approaches to it started to silt up a small town was established on the east side of the harbour. Richard I granted it borough status in 1194, and the town began to concentrate on shipbuilding, although it never really flourished, largely no doubt because Southampton maintained legal control of it as a port. However, its naval base potential was beginning to be realized in the fifteenth century, and Henry V probably built some of its first defences. The Round Tower dates from 1418, followed by the Square Tower at the end of the century. Henry VII established Britain's first dry dock at Portsmouth in 1495, but it was Henry VIII who not only improved the city's defences but also founded the first royal dockyard in 1540. During peace-time, according to Leland, Tudor Portsmouth was "bare and little occupied", but the seventeenth century saw Charles I and Cromwell enlarging it, and by Charles II's time it was England's chief naval base, a position maintained ever since. Pepys found it "a very pleasant and strong place", a description which is not out of place today.

The eighteenth century saw the town expand into Portsea, between Old Town and the Dockyard, and the fact that it has been a garrison town from Napoleonic times onwards has resulted in a steady surge of Portsmouth's growth, so that the island site filled up, and eventually the sprawl on to the mainland became inevitable. Almost all this represented natural growth, haphazard and unplanned; unfortunately, the large amount of rebuilding following bomb damage during the second war seems to have continued this piecemeal theme. It is not, therefore, in its modern guise that Portsmouth's appeal lies, but in its defence works, its naval and military structures of the eighteenth and nineteenth centuries, and some domestic buildings around the Old Town areas of High Street, Broad Street and the Sally Port. Here are echoes of the town that Nelson knew, but modern Portsmouth has migrated towards Commercial Road, where Charles Dickens's house contains many mementoes of the novelist's life and work. But Portsmouth's heart remains in the dockyards, symbolized by HMS *Victory*, built in 1765, Nelson's flagship at Trafalgar, and now surrounded by naval sheds of red brick and concrete. Portsmouth's twin town of Southsea provides a resort side to the older town's character, with a sand and shingle beach, the usual amusements, a sixteenth-century fort now housing a museum, and a fine broad promenade from which to look across Spithead to the Isle of Wight.

To the east the freaky, natural phenomenon of Hayling Island separates the tidal waters of Langstone Harbour from Chichester Harbour, with a bridge at Havant linking it to the mainland. Sandy beaches and a very warm climate make it the focus for summer's sun-seeking crowds, yet its history goes back to the Conquest, when William gave Hayling Island to the Abbey of Jumièges, in Normandy, and a priory was built, only to be destroyed by inundation in 1324. Altogether, the sea has eroded the island's size to about ten square miles.

Whereas at Portsmouth the military and naval elements of the city are, if anything, declining in size and importance, while communications to London are improving, so that it is now within commuting distance, away to the west Southampton shows an entirely different story, historically as well as at the present time.

Southampton gives its name to the county. A Saxon charter names it as Hamtun, from which emerges Hamtunscir, but the area was settled much earlier, by the Romans, at Bitterne on the other side of the Itchen. In 1016 Cnut was offered the English crown at Southampton, and after the Conquest the town obviously became one of the most important ports of embarkation for the continent. From its harbour armies sailed to the Crusades, to the French battlefields of Crécy and Agincourt, while incomers from across the Channel included Philip II of Spain, on his way to marry Queen Mary I, and the Emperor Charles V. During medieval times it

Southampton: Bargate was originally the north gate of the medieval walled town.

developed as a trading port, shipping wool across the water, and importing French wines. It suffered seaborne attacks in 1334 by Spanish and Genoese vessels, which plundered the town, and as the wool trade declined during the sixteenth century, so did Southampton's fortunes. As Portsmouth grew in naval importance the following century, a serious outbreak of plague in 1665 further helped to diminish Southampton's stature, so that by the time of the first census of 1801 it had fewer than 8,000 inhabitants, less than a quarter of Portsmouth's population.

But the Napoleonic Wars saw it revitalized as an embarkation port for British armies, and the discovery of a small spa in 1750 helped to stimulate it as a small fashionable resort with theatre and assembly rooms. Visitors to the town then included Pope, Swift and Horace Walpole, while later, between 1806 and 1809, Jane Austen and her mother lived in a large house, now vanished, in a corner of Castle Square. The buildings remaining from this more elegant heyday are loosely scattered beyond the medieval town walls, for the extensive town fields caused this early nineteenth-century expansion to be sketchy in plan, and the fields subsequently became the spacious parks of Victorian times. But there was nothing of Georgian or Regency days to match, even fractionally, what had happened at Brighton and Cheltenham.

In 1840 the railway from London reached the town, followed in two years by the opening of the first dock. Victorian and Edwardian growth of commerce, trade and further docks saw Southampton's population grow to 35,000 in 1851, and 105,000 fifty years later. Now it has more than doubled again. Its watering-place nature was transferred to Bournemouth so that it is as Britain's main passenger seaport that Southampton now is so proud. I'm sure the best approach to it is by water, conveniently enjoyed by the frequent little ferry from Hythe, on the opposite side of Southampton Water, which brings you into the heart of the docks, with splendid views of ocean-liners and the paraphernalia which constitutes the great waterfront scene.

Better still, as soon as you cross the road from the ferry terminal you see some of the medieval town. It is this historical aspect of Southampton which puts it close to England's other cities with extensive medieval remains, York and Chester. Extensive bomb damage failed to destroy much of the old walls, so that you can see today God's House Gate, Westgate, the Water Gate and other medieval towers. The River Test formerly lapped the town walls where the busy Western Esplanade runs outside them on land reclaimed from the estuary, and you can walk along the ramparts above the hum of traffic. Town walls, castle wall, a sentry walk, the Arcades and fragments of a Norman house march side by side with the twentieth century, while the fourteenth-century Wool House, splendidly restored and proudly displaying its old roof timbers of Spanish chestnut, now houses a fine maritime museum,

Overleaf: *Portsmouth Harbour, from the medieval Round Tower.*

with the rare virtue of free admission. Southampton's theme of old and new is appropriately demonstrated where its main thoroughfare, High Street, meets Bargate Street. Bargate itself acts as a traffic roundabout, but it was originally the north gate of the walled town.

At the head of Southampton Water was the old port of Elling, which grew northwards into Totton, primarily an industrial complex of the later nineteenth century, with chaotic additions of houses and factories ever since. Wessex seems a million miles away, yet a few minutes' drive takes you through New Forest country towards Lyndhurst, with the A337 subsequently leading southwards, passing a series of good eighteenth-century milestones, to Lymington, a little gem of a town on the west bank of the tidal Lymington river. A forest of masts denotes its growth as one of the south coast's busiest yachting marinas. Saturday sees the nicely sloping High Street lively with stalls, a reminder that a market charter was granted as long ago as 1150, when the town was an important port and shipbuilding centre. Salt added an extra source of prosperity, obtained from 'salterns' in small creeks to the south. Sea-water was allowed to fill tidal ponds, then admitted to evaporating pans for boiling, the whole process taking about four months. During the seventeenth and eighteenth centuries the trade was at its peak, and large quantities of salt were shipped to London. A severe salt tax, and cheaper salt from Worcestershire and Cheshire, killed the industry, and only a few buildings remain including the Chequers Inn, formerly used by the salt tax collectors.

Lymington is a place to savour, catching flavours of Georgian elegance, from the top of High Street, where the cupola on the parish church tower is rightly an indication of good things inside, to cobbled Quay Hill and the narrow streets near the waterfront. Bow windows and busts, inns and yacht chandlers, contribute to Lymington's appeal. The folk who use the town merely as a departure-point for the Isle of Wight ferry miss a lot – even though they do obtain a splendid panorama of masts and moorings from down the estuary.

A quiet evening at Lymington, Hampshire.

Four miles south-west of Lymington, Milford-on-Sea is a late Victorian development as a resort with a shingle beach, good bathing and a rare mid-nineteenth-century pillar-box. Hurst Castle, at the eastern end of a long spit of beach, is one of a chain of castles built by Henry VIII, with its inner fortress a twelve-sided tower. The two brick, but stone-fronted, wings which now frame the castle date from 1873, and the whole building (Department of the Environment) justifies the walk along the foreshore to visit it. Between Milford and Christchurch, Barton-on-Sea doesn't justify very much at all, and Christchurch, transferred from Hampshire, now forms one of three district councils within the huge urban spread, the other two being Bournemouth and Poole.

Christchurch is cunningly situated on a triangle of land between the Rivers Avon and Stour, just above their meeting-point at the head of Christchurch Harbour. Position and priory have given prominence to Christchurch, but of the old town itself there is not a great deal. If you climb the steep-sided artificial motte of the castle, just above the bowling-green, you see what little remains of the castle masonry, ruined east and west walls; but there is a magnificent view of Christchurch Priory, which reveals its incredible length, as well as its very fragmented profile, completely out of proportion. Yet when you go into the church, the effect of its great length is impressive in the extreme, with seven Norman arcades making up a nave 118 feet long. Medieval wood-carvings, stone reredos and chantries, paintings by Millais and a white marble monument to Shelley, all very beautiful, play second fiddle to the Norman detail of the north transept. To the north-west of the church the Red House, an early Georgian building of red brick which was originally the parish workhouse, now houses a museum and art gallery.

Westwards across the Stour, Bournemouth begins, and arcs gently round ten miles of bay, from Hengistbury Head in the east to Sandbanks in the west. Before 1810 much of the country between Christchurch Harbour and Poole Harbour was open heathland, with merely a scatter of villages and steep-sided valleys

Lymington: Quay Hill, a cobbled street with Georgian buildings.

leading down to the sea. Then in 1810 Lewis Tregonwell built himself a house on the edge of such a valley, its site now incorporated into the Royal Exeter Hotel. An inn, a few cottages for servants, houses for his relatives and friends, completed this first little Bournemouth. After Tregonwell died in 1834 a colony of detached villas was added to the east side of the Bourne valley. Called Westover Villas, this was planned as a winter health resort, and more plantations of pine trees were added to those which Tregonwell had planted. Carefully placed detached houses were gradually added, without disturbing the wooded nature of the landscape, but the inevitable result was a sprawling, formless little town whose population in 1851 was fewer than 700. By 1870 the railway line from the Midlands reached Bournemouth, and by 1890 the population had reached 37,000. Since then it has more than quadrupled in size, and large blocks of flats replace many of the Victorian villas. The pines, the chines, steeply-rising cliffs, parks, gardens, heathlands, amusements, esplanades, sands and sprawl, add up to the strange, unique character of Bournemouth. A fascinating, pine-scented phenomenon, somewhat updated from Hardy's description of it, as Sandbourne in *Tess of the d'Urberville's*, as a "city of detached mansions".

From Sandbanks to South Haven Point about 400 yards of water is the only opening to the sea from Poole's almost land-locked harbour, nearly a hundred miles round, with channels winding among mud-flats which dry out at low tide, and seven permanent islands besides. The main channel round the east of Brownsea Island has been deepened to take ships up to 3,500 tons, with vessels bringing in timber and coal for the gas-works and power station at Hamworthy, and taking away malt barley and feeding stuffs. Whereas Bournemouth represents a mushroom of growth, concentrated in time, scattered in disarray, Poole's story spans seven centuries, but its heathwards sprawl is a little more planned, if still scarring the Dorset landscape. As Wareham declined during the thirteenth century through the River Frome silting up, so Poole emerged on land owned by William Longespee in Canford parish, obtaining its borough charter in 1248. Three centuries later it was granted county status, and from the sixteenth century onwards its

The view towards Studland from Ballard Down on the chalk ridge. Poole harbour and Brownsea Island can be seen in the distance.

prosperity was largely based on the fishing fleet specializing in cod from Newfoundland waters, and the resulting trade which this engendered. Wool was always its chief export, and the fifteenth-century Wool House, or Town Cellars, now being restored, is one of two survivors of an early importance, the other being Scaplen's Court.

Poole's nucleus was around its triangular market-place, where the Guildhall of 1761 makes such an attractive focus, with Market Street and Church Street running southwards from it. Parallel with it and to the east is High Street, leading towards Strand Street, whose name suggests that it once lay at the waterside. Now narrow lanes link it to The Quay, showing that the shoreline has been pushed back a short way, and warehouses built on the land so

The Guildhall, Poole, built in 1761.

gained. After about 1820, Poole's fishing trade fell away, at the same time as Bournemouth was stirring into being, and with the growth of the newer town acting almost as a magnet, so did Poole gradually move its centre eastwards, a process which continued for a century, culminating in the establishment of an administrative centre at Poole Park in the 1930s. But the older Poole stayed around The Quay. Merchants' houses of Georgian brick reflect the good trading days, but lesser houses have been lost, so that much of Poole's heart has gone. Replacements are not inspiring, and on the whole it is better to concentrate nearer the waterside scene, with the Custom House, Harbour Office, Mansion House, and Poole's most attractive street, Church Street. Along The Quay is the modern factory and showroom of Poole Pottery, founded in 1873, where you can enjoy a guided tour, or merely feast your eyes on an excellent and varied display.

Inland, Poole sprawls redly. Across the water, however, is Brownsea Island, now owned by the National Trust and visited by over 100,000 people annually. They land by cottages on a quay-side, and soon enter heath and woodland, with marshes and quiet beaches, comprising a 500-acre nature reserve in stark contrast to the urban mainland little over a mile away. Cerne Abbey monks owned the island in the sixth century; Henry VIII built a castle there in the 1540s to guard Poole Harbour, on the site of the present castle; in later years a number of eccentric owners have made their own marks on Brownsea, not least of them Mrs Mary Christie. From 1927 to 1961 she lived there almost alone, except for a gamekeeper and a blonde Scandinavian woman whose power was sufficient to keep away intruders. Mrs Christie allowed the island to become a haven for wild life, and when the Trust took it over much of Brownsea was almost a wilderness. This was in sharp contrast to the years at the beginning of this century, when Charles van Raalte owned Brownsea and maintained a staff of thirty at the castle. During that time, his friend General Baden-Powell persuaded him to allow a summer camp to be held there for twenty boys. In 1907 the Boy Scouts Association came into being, and if for no other reason than this, Brownsea Island deserves an honourable mention in the story of Wessex and of England.

Southwards are the heaths of Purbeck, showing chalky cliffs to the sea. Beyond them the coast stretches westwards to the Devon boundary, and except for an area around Portland and Weymouth, forms the Channel frontier of an Area of Outstanding Natural Beauty designated in 1957, and comprising nearly 40 per cent of all Dorset. Few coastlines in Britain are so varied, with natural beauty matching outstanding geological interest, where all the strata of the Jurassic series of rocks are revealed. At Foreland, near Swanage, Purbeck's spiny ridge of chalk ends in the stark accents of vertical pinnacles, echoing The Needles on the Isle of Wight, and illustrating how these two sets of stacks are the remaining portals of the great breach made by the sea when it penetrated a land barrier to make the Solent and Poole Harbour. Further west the sea made smaller invasions of the coast at Worbarrow Bay and Lulworth Cove, overcoming the resistant limestones to reach and attack the softer strata behind them.

Swanage, Weymouth and Lyme Regis are the only towns along this coast, each having a story to tell. That of Swanage is the simplest. Throughout medieval times it was never more than a small fishing village from which small quantities of Purbeck marble were also transported. In 1821 there were sixty quarries working in the parish but before the end of the eighteenth century a local landowner had tried to emulate the resort attractions of Weymouth and Lyme Regis, but without much success. A further attempt in 1825 proved more rewarding, Marine Villas and neighbouring terraces were built, the High Street was a mile long, and Swanage became a quietly fashionable resort favoured by professional people, no doubt helped by the railways' arrival in 1881, bringing in its wake the usual addition of Victorian hotels. Swanage's present character is largely of that period, helped by the eccentric local contractor George Burt who was responsible for, among other buildings, the Town Hall, the Grosvenor Hotel and Durlston Castle. This latter is now the nucleus of a Country Park of 261 acres, opened by Dorset County Council in 1973, to conserve the area for public enjoyment. A derelict radar camp has been landscaped into car parks and most of the unsightly overhead power cables have been put underground. The fine cliffs from Durlston

A wall of Purbeck stone near Worth Matravers, Dorset.

Head to Tilly Whim Caves are a wild-life sanctuary, and a Warden Service located at the Information Centre aims to manage the Country Park and help the visiting public to gain most from its attractions.

North of Swanage Studland marks the beginning of Britain's longest footpath. The South-West Peninsula Coast Path, planned by the Countryside Commission to run for 515 miles from Studland to Minehead, is not yet a total reality, but it is possible to follow coastal and cliff-top tracks for almost the whole way, with rights of access. Except for a section near Abbotsbury, you can walk the length of the Dorset coast, but most people are far more likely to explore it in short sections, using villages on or near the coast as points of access. The magnificent Purbeck coast has only two such places, Worth Matravers and Kimmeridge, where a toll road leads down to the little harbour, and the shaly platform of the

179

shore is a chaos of tumbled stones and boulders, a place full of atmosphere and fossils, and, slightly inland, having the prospect of oil wells.

Westwards lies the Army-dominated stretch of coast, around Tyneham and Worbarrow, where cliffs of great beauty form a backcloth to barbed wire, derelict and battered barns, and the occasional courtesy of public access. Nature has done well, however, as a result of people being kept out. One presumes the military have no interest in wild life, so it survives undisturbed. More army restrictions exist at Lulworth, but once the famous Cove is passed, a sense of freedom returns, and the great bay at Weymouth sweeps round to the extending finger of Portland Bill.

After Brighton, Melcombe Regis, now incorporated into Weymouth, is the best example of a Georgian and Regency seaside resort. Both towns were founded in the fourteenth century, grew as busy medieval ports, rivalling each other in woollen exports, but then slowly decayed as Poole began to flourish. Then in 1748 the new fashions in sea-bathing started a revival in their fortunes, and when in 1780 the Duke of Gloucester wintered at Melcombe, and built a fine house there, prosperity was assured. George III set the seal on this after his visits during the 1790s and early 1800s, and Melcombe's size and social standing grew accordingly. You can measure its northward expansion in the names of streets and terraces. The handsome Esplanade started in 1785, Gloucester Row five years later, and Royal Crescent in the 1800s. Even when the royal visits ended in 1811, growth continued, with Royal Terrace built in 1816, Brunswick Terrace in the 1820s, Frederick Place and Waterloo Place in the 1830s, and Victoria Terrace about 1850. Three generations of middle- and upper-class housing at Melcombe reflect as well as anywhere in England the changing materials and façades of the decades from 1780 to 1850. I find them much more absorbing than the great golden curve of sand which has drawn visitors to Melcombe for nearly two centuries. Weymouth, on a more restricted site south of the river, developed less fashionably, but to an equally prosperous extent, until the 1850s, when building slowed down at both places. Later Victorian growth and modern developments, to say nothing of the huge caravan sites, have savaged the hinterland, emphasizing again that non-industrial development can be worse than factory complexes, especially on or near the coast. At least an industrial skyline has some character and its buildings are more concentrated.

Hardy's Budmouth Regis features in a number of stories and poems, *The Trumpet Major, Desperate Remedies, The Rivals* and *The Dynasts* among them, while *The Well Beloved* has many references to the 'Isle of Slingers', known to us as the Isle of Portland. This strangely formidable area is a huge lump of limestone over four miles long and a mile wide, dramatic in profile, distinctive in character, mainly because, except in the neighbourhood of Pennsylvania Castle, it has no trees, and a landscape without trees is generally bare and friendless. For centuries Portland has been one huge quarry, its stone having been used for building since medieval times, reaching its peak from the seventeenth century onwards. Inigo Jones and later Wren used it extensively for great London buildings and churches, and millions of tons of Portland stone was shipped away, either directly from cliffside quarries or from small jetties such as that at Church Ope Cove.

Quarries still operate, although today's demand for pure Portland stone has diminished, and a reconstituted composite, 'Portcrete', is commonly used. Cuboid boulders are piled high by derrick-guarded workings, or litter the shore-line. Rock platforms are fine viewpoints at the island's tip, from which to look at the sheltered anchorage of Portland Roads, the curving coast of Weymouth Bay, and westwards the freakishly fascinating Chesil Beach. Since Hardy's day, Portland's appearance has probably changed rather less than its functions. The railway to Portland has been closed to passengers, the little station demolished, and now ranks of silvery fuel tanks stand beside the line. The infantry garrison has been replaced by the Ministry of Defence, with Henry VIII's Portland Castle partially incorporated into it, Verne Citadel of 1860 is now a prison, the Victorian prison a Borstal, Pennsylvania Castle an hotel, but St George, Reforme, remains the finest Georgian church in Dorset, possibly in Wessex.

Portland is linked to the mainland by the Chesil Beach, eight miles away at Abbotsbury, flanked for most of this length by a lagoon called The Fleet. Chesil is unique in Europe, an enormous reef of clay on which rounded pebbles of flint have constantly been rolled and hurled by the tides from the south-west, with Portland Bill acting as a gigantic groyne preventing their further eastward movement. Graded in size from pea to fist, west to east, this natural sea wall of shingle has been the haunt of wreckers, the ultimate landing place of exotic sea creatures and strange flotsam from across the oceans. The innermost sanctuary of The Fleet has housed a swannery since at least the fourteenth century, having been established by the important Benedictine monastery at Abbotsbury. A thousand swans and their cygnets attract thousands of visitors who are obviously prepared to tolerate the pungent smell for close-range views of the proud white swans, a few wild geese and duck. Of the abbey itself most traces have vanished, apart from gatehouse fragments and the splendid Abbey Barn, one of the longest in England, dating from about 1400, but with a later timber roof. In the summer-busy village raised pavements add their own distinction to the two main streets of honey-coloured terraced cottages, many thatched and mostly of the seventeenth and eighteenth centuries. At the northern end of Market Street a triangular open space was obviously the market-place in Abbotsbury's busier days.

The road to Bridport climbs for a mile out of the village, and from thoughtfully placed laybys at the top, near the Iron Age hill-fort of Abbotsbury Castle, there are magnificent views eastwards along the length of the Chesil Beach, to Portland Bill beyond, while westwards are Burton Bradstock, the cliffs of West Bay and in the distance, Golden Cap.

Burton Bradstock is a large, welcoming village, sheltering in the Bride valley, with its best parts lying just off the main road. Recent additions have been inland rather than seawards, but there is a very conspicuous caravan site to the west, preparing you, as it were, for the worse intrusions around West Bay, now the port and quay for Bridport itself. Roads almost totally enclose the small harbour, built in 1740–44, and rebuilt eighty years later; now popular with the messing-about-in-boats fraternity. Sand and shingle beaches are backed by vertical cliffs of an orangy-coloured sandstone.

Burton Bradstock, Dorset.

Tourism having affected West Bay, Bridport itself has managed to escape its worse ravages, and remains one of Dorset's least-mangled towns, with a wealth of good, if unspectacular, buildings in its main streets.

The main A35 passes through the centre of the town, heading westwards for Chideock, Charmouth and Lyme Regis, but leaving

Overleaf: *Old Harry Rocks, near Studland, Dorset.*

the best part of the Wessex coast to the National Trust and the walker. Recognizing the Heritage quality of this stretch, the Trust has gradually acquired, since 1961, 1,600 acres of the Golden Cap Estate between Eype Bay and Charmouth. A band of bright orange sandstone, table-topped, with a jutting profile to the sea, identifies the centre of this complex of country, Golden Cap, well-named, and at 619 feet the highest land along the south coast. Around it is farmland, woodland, gorse-covered common, complementing the natural beauties of cliff and beach. In addition to the coast path, bridleways and footpaths encourage exploration, and National Trust holiday cottages offer opportunities for longer stays. Beech clumps on inland hills are said to have been landmarks for brandy-smuggling boats of the eighteenth century, and rocky coves at the base of the cliffs, accessible on foot only at low tide, were useful storage places for the contraband. Walk anywhere on these open places, Doghouse Hill, Stonebarrow Hill, Thorncombe Beacon or Golden Cap, with a wind from the sea on a late spring day, and you feel that this is one of the best places in all Wessex, and say a quiet thanksgiving for Enterprise Neptune which has enabled it to remain so.

Of Charmouth Jane Austen wrote that "it was the happiest spot for watching the flow of the tide, for sitting in unwearied contemplation". Traffic then was coaches which stopped at one or other of its inns. The Queen's Arms is Tudor inside behind its Regency frontage, and the name commemorates Catherine of Aragon who is said to have stayed there in 1501. After the Battle of Worcester in 1651 the fugitive Prince Charles hid there while waiting for a boat to take him to France. Charmouth's Regency bow-windows, thatch and colour-wash are far-removed from the estates and caravan sites along the road to the beach half a mile away. To the west the cliffs of Black Venn are National Trust property, leased to the Dorset Naturalists' Trust as a nature reserve, primarily for their rich fossil content. Geological fame came to Black Venn in 1811 when twelve-year-old Mary Anning found the famous ichthyosaurus which now occupies an honoured place on the shelves of the

Lyme Regis: the sea-front between the town and the Cobb.

South Kensington Natural History Museum.

From east or west you descend steep hills into Lyme Regis, which was recorded in Domesday Book as a small village, but developed as a result of the building of a breakwater called the Cobb, at the end of the thirteenth century. This was the only safe anchorage along an inhospitable coastline, and soon helped Lyme to prosper; Edward I gave it a charter in 1295, but repeated damage by the sea wrecked the Cobb a century later. It was duly rebuilt, more than once, but attacks by French raiders continued to give it a rather chequered history. It seems to have been a fishing and trading port in Tudor times; in 1588 it looked out to a minor skirmish between Drake's fleet and the Spanish Armada; 1644 saw it last out for two months against a strong royalist siege; and in 1685 the Duke of Monmouth landed near the Cobb at the start of his ill-fated rebellion.

In the late eighteenth century a Mr Hollis bought an inn and some houses, persuaded Lord Chatham to stay, and Lyme's renaissance as a seaside resort was under way. Bath's fashionable society visitors included Jane Austen, who features it in *Persuasion*, and obviously preferred the Cobb to the town itself. Contemporary with Melcombe Regis, Lyme is much more intimate, less grand, and although Broad Street has good Classical frontages above the shops, behind them are older interior structures. Middle Row encroaches at the bottom of the street, doubtless occupying the old market space, and behind it the Esplanade leads past cottages and villas to the Cobb. Ammonites from nearby Blue Lias cliffs decorate walls, a yacht chandler's does brisk business, an 1830 bonded warehouse is a reminder of earlier trade, and the harbour, though full, usually finds room for an extra yacht or two, which is more than car parks can manage. With the Devon border only half a mile away, the Cobb at Lyme Regis is a good place at which to end, or begin, a view of the Wessex coast.

From the Wessex coastline east of Swanage, and from Portland Bill, the Isle of Wight is a prominent if not dominant, feature. Its position creates the double high tide so useful to Southampton, its high chalk downs are an extension of those on the mainland, its sheltered chines – they would be combes in the West Country –

appealed to early Victorian tastes for the picturesque, and the resorts built last century continue to attract thousands of visitors, most of whom make for the sandy beaches, the sunny 'honey-pot' spots, the picture-postcard villages like Winkle Street and Gods-hill. Cowes is Britain's yachting centre, but Yarmouth has more history and atmosphere. Ventnor's terraces, Shanklin's chine, Ryde's pier and popularity, Carisbrooke's Castle, all help to spread the summer loads, but out of season you can drive round the island in a morning, walk on the cliffs or the downs, and look across the Channel, or along to the chalk stacks of Studland, without ever feeling that you are in Wessex. There is merely a view of the Wessex coast from across a few miles of water, and I for one am happier to be on the mainland, closer to the mainstream of Wessex life, history and literature.

Dorset heathlands near Wareham — sands, pools, pines, birches, where man has made little impression on the landscape.

CHAPTER 6

THE LAND–DOWNS, FORESTS AND HEATH

THERE IS SCARCELY any part of the Wessex landscape that has not been changed by man. Two hundred generations of cultural humus lie on its chalk uplands which comprise about two-thirds of its total area. Forty or fifty generations have cultivated its vales, drained its low-lying moors, cleared woods and forests, but the greatest changes of all have occurred in little more than one generation, in the three decades since 1940. These have affected the downland most of all.

Three centuries ago a Wiltshireman, John Aubrey, wrote of the appeal of downland. "The turfe is of short sweet grasse, good for the sheep, and delightful to the traveller; for here is . . . not a tree, or rarely a bush to shelter one from a shower". Woodlands from some of the vales extended only partly up the hillsides so that the higher land was bare. Not until the eighteenth century, with its enclosure acts and landscape planning, did the familiar hill-crest beech clumps and hillside shelter-belts add their darker shapes to the clean outlines of downland.

Farming life on the Wessex Downs has ebbed and flowed through the centuries. Prehistoric occupation has already been referred to, and it is known that communities existed on the chalk through Roman times and the Dark Ages until the coming of the Saxons who settled in the vales. But they grazed the downs with their stock, for Domesday Book gives evidence of some sizes of flocks, 1,600 sheep at Puddletown and 1,000 at Cranborne for instance. Use of downland for sheep walks continued until the early 1300s, but from then onwards human settlement on the downs contracted, for various reasons, one of which was concerned with the visitations of plague between 1340 and 1380, while other causes of depopulation were the gradual loss of soil fertility after 4,000 years of husbandry, and the change in the chalk's water-table arising from clearances of lower land-levels and valley settlement. Throughout Wessex during the fourteenth and fifteenth centuries the downs lost much of their arable nature and became even more intensive grazing grounds. Sheep flocks increased, their nibbling teeth keeping at bay the ever-threatening scrub, living lawn-mowers of the short, sweet turf.

Downland sheep are short-wool breeds. Dorset Horns are one of the oldest British breeds, and tend to be restricted, so far as Wessex is concerned, to the south of Dorset and Somerset, and the Isle of Wight. They have the unique ability to breed at any time of the year, with the advantage of being mated in April or May to produce late autumn lambs in time to be fattened for Christmas. Hampshire Downs, which have dark faces and are hornless, have evolved from the downland flocks of centuries ago, though actually a cross breed recognized in 1861, Wiltshire with a South-down, yielding a very high quality lambswool.

All the early travellers commented on the sheep, Leland in 1540, Camden in 1580, while Defoe, in 1724, suggested there were 600,000 within six miles of Dorchester. A single farm at Sydling St Nicholas had 2,700 sheep in 1550. Numbers such as these could only be managed and controlled by enclosing areas of open downland into large rectangular fields, a process which went on, first by private agreement, and later by Acts of Parliament, until the end of the eighteenth century, after which the Napoleonic Wars gave an extra impetus towards enclosure, and some downland was temporarily ploughed. Certainly by about 1840 almost the whole of the Wessex Downs had been divided by hedges into the large enclosed fields which today pattern their rolling uplands. Generally, these new fields were still worked from farms in the villages, but increasingly groups of barns and sheds were built, usually around

The view north-west from the Ridgeway, above Avebury, Wiltshire. Lansdowne Column, Cherhill can be seen on the skyline. The sheep are Hampshire Downs.

yards, in the middle of a large area of fields, and these focused much farming activity. Though some are now derelict others have been replaced by modern structures, and many are named on the Ordnance Survey maps.

Scattered barns, especially the large modern ones, are the only angular accents on the broad curves of downland. Colours are pastel, muted, nothing harsh, and the flowers of the chalk are small, fewer now in number as the numbers of sheep have diminished. They trimmed the grasses, allowing flowers to flourish, milkwort, eyebrights, tormentil, wild thyme, bird's-foot trefoil, harebell, viper's bugloss, scabious, carline thistle and orchids. Tufty anthills pock-marked the surface, and butterflies abounded, as they still do in good dry seasons, chalk-hill blue, small blues, heaths, skippers, marbled whites, fritillaries.

Although the downlands of Wessex, especially Salisbury Plain, had felt the impact of the Army long before the First World War, it was the Second War that brought most revolutionary changes. Mechanization, chemical fertilizers, and restricted imports which demanded more food production in Britain combined to bring about a great transformation. The thin chalk soil previously thought to be of little arable worth was ploughed up, thousands of acres of grain were sown and successfully harvested. New-style enclosure by post-and-rail fence brought into use hundreds of smaller fields, and as the short grass disappeared so did much of the wild life, flowers, butterflies and birds. Ironically, only on some of the army lands which were not ploughed did the former fauna survive in any quantity. Elsewhere, the downland edges, too steep for ploughing, remained unaltered, and little grazed, so scrub tended to invade them, creating new habitats for wild life.

The changes in farming have brought changes in colour. Whereas turf stayed green throughout the year, arable land is bare during winter, green in spring and early summer, golden as the corn ripens to harvest and the succeeding stubble, when the white and flinty bones show through again. Perhaps these changing facets of downland are compensation for the loss of sheep and wild flowers, but I find it very sad to reflect that they are the outcome of a society which measures everything in terms of economics. Barley gives a better financial return than sheep, so let us plough up the grass; the agricultural equivalent of the rent-collecting blocks of brick and concrete which have shaken the soul out of towns. The old Chinese proverb seems forgotten: "If you have two pennies to spend, spend one on a loaf of bread and the other on a flower. The first will give you the means of life, the second a reason for living."

All is not completely lost. Here and there nature reserves have been established, either by the Nature Conservancy Council or by County Naturalist Trusts. Fyfield Down, between Avebury and Marlborough, covers 612 acres of chalk downland; Pewsey Down, also in Wiltshire, extends over 188 acres on the slopes of Knap Hill; while on the Hampshire chalk Old Winchester Hill's 140 acres include two nature trails. Complementing these national nature reserves, where downland wild life is zealously conserved, the National Trust in 1976 has acquired 150 acres of Fontmell Down, south of Shaftesbury, as an appropriate memorial to Thomas Hardy. The management plan for Fontmell Down includes grazing by cattle and Dorset Horn sheep, provided by Anthony Kay of Melbury Abbas, so that in one small corner of the county a fraction of its former 70,000 downland acres are saved for future generations to appreciate what chalkland pasture is like. Westwards is Blackmore Vale, with a dim skyline of more distant downs beyond, a shimmering view which has hardly changed since the days of Hardy's youth.

In Hampshire east and west from Old Winchester Hill is a landscape of isolated rounded hills which, unlike most of Wiltshire's chalklands, have no steep scarp face. Much of this high land is remarkably bare, but splendid stands of beeches clothe the hillsides, and there are few villages between the Itchen and the Meon valleys, immediately south of the A272 Winchester–Petersfield road. Butser Hill marks the eastern end of this range of hills, as well as the highest, a point regrettably proved by the hideous telecommunications aerial now disfiguring it. However, by turning your back on metalscape you are rewarded by magnificent views from the summit ridge of Butser. The busy Portsmouth road cuts across its eastern flanks, with War Down beyond, where trees planted by the Forestry Commission in 1928 have now matured. 860 acres of woodlands were named the Queen Elizabeth Forest Park in 1953, and more recently, joint efforts by Hampshire County Council and the Forestry Commission have linked Butser and the woods in a 1,325-acre Country Park, with the contrasting attractions of woodland rides and open downland. A westward extension of the South Down Way continues to Winchester, although the Countryside Commission's first long-distance footpath and bridleway originally ended at Sunwood Farm just on the Hampshire side of the Sussex border, where Wessex can also be said to end. The bridleway is nevertheless a timely reminder that the best of Wessex lies off the roads, along field and riverside paths, through heaths and woodlands, along the coast and on the ancient downland tracks.

The chalky uplands of Wessex have inspired some of our finest natural history writing. Although he is usually associated with Sussex, W. H. Hudson stayed at Martin, a downland village in south Wiltshire with cob and thatch cottages, while gathering material for one of his most descriptive books, *A Shepherd's Life*. Based on the village which he renamed Winterbourne Bishop, this portrays Wiltshire downland at the early part of this century. West of the village, Martin Down is one of the few remaining chalkland commons in Wessex.

Richard Jefferies was born in 1848, seven years after Hudson, but died when he was only thirty-nine. His birthplace and boyhood home was Coate Farm on the southern outskirts of Swindon, greatly altered since then, but with its top floor now housing a museum. Nearby, Coate Water was a well-loved spot, a large pool constructed as a reservoir for the Wiltshire and Berkshire Canal, and now owned by Swindon Corporation. Jefferies' greatest delight, however, was to walk on the downs near his home where one of his favourite places was the southern edge of Barbury Castle. With a view over the broad plain, enclosed by an amphitheatre of green hills, farmhouses hidden by trees and woods, he could be alone with the sun and the air, and experience bouts of mystical emotion, identifying himself with the physical world,

Old Winchester Hill, Hampshire, a National Nature Reserve.

from the earth's firmness to the songs of chaffinches and the great blue bowl of the sky.

Edward Thomas, born thirty years later than Jefferies, was killed in 1917 in Flanders. This university-educated historian, naturalist, artist and poet walked on the downs seeking, and finding, solitude. He liked secret lanes and long-forgotten tracks, was always moved by the shapes of trees and hills, the glory of clouds, the grouping of houses in villages, and he had the observer's eye for the life of hedgerows and fields. His greatest walk was the length of the Icknield Way, from Thetford in Norfolk to Wanborough, by Swindon, its course being to the north of the Ridgeway, and usually just above the spring line near the foot of the North Wessex Downs. These three naturalist-writers found on the windy uplands wider horizons of feeling, their own crocks of gold beneath the rainbows, the sudden glories of unobstructed views from edges of downland where even a modest height brings a sense of freedom and elation. They have a lesson for us today.

Downland villages are few and far between. Many were deserted between the fourteenth and sixteenth centuries, but Imber, in the middle of Salisbury Plain, was evacuated in 1943, at the Army's demand. Naturally it was to be only a temporary expedient. Naturally it has become permanent. Its houses are ruined by shelling, mock battles and practice street-fighting, and there is barbed wire round the church, where a service is held once a year. Occasionally the public are allowed to drive or walk to Imber, but it is a forlorn and depressing pilgrimage. Much better is it to visit Buttermere, on the Wiltshire–Berkshire border, at about 700 feet Wiltshire's highest village. A few miles to the west is Wexcombe, home of Mr A. J. Hosier, who in the bad farming times of 1930 introduced the idea of the Hosier milking bail, and gate-like sections of barbed-wire fences, which improved downland farming.

Wessex is 'white horse' country, possessing nine of the dozen such figures which Britain can muster (the others are in Sussex, Yorkshire and Scotland). Chalk escarpments have been a great temptation to large-scale landscape artists, and in addition to its

Westbury White Horse, Wiltshire.

white horses Wessex has a number of other intaglio hill-figures.

Pride of place for antiquity and fluidity of line must go to the Uffington horse, an impressively simple figure believed to have been cut in the first century B.C. The Westbury horse in west Wiltshire, modelled in 1778 and now surfaced with a thin chalky concrete, casts a baleful eye on the huge cement works at the foot of the downs. Cherhill's horse looks across the A4 east of Calne, and dates from 1780, probably about the same age as the tiny Woolbury horse, near Stockbridge in Hampshire, a flint-outlined figure on the ramparts of Woolbury Camp. Wiltshire's other horses are at Alton Barnes, 1812, Broad Town, near Wootton Bassett, 1864, Hackpen Hill, 1838, and Marlborough, 1804, while Pewsey's 'new' horse was a 1937 replacement of a much older animal. Dorset's only horse at Osmington is unique in having a rider, supposedly George III, and probably dates from the early nineteenth century, commemorating the King's fondness for Weymouth.

During the 1914–18 war soldiers stationed at local camps cut a number of regimental badges in the chalk hillsides above the Nadder valley, at Fovant, Compton Chamberlayne and Sutton Mandeville. From 1949 to 1951 new badges were cut and old ones restored, and this unusual piece of military history now contains eleven well-tended badges. At Beacon Hill near Bulford, New Zealand troops cut an enormous kiwi, and at Laverstock, near Salisbury, Britain's newest chalk figure depicts a panda, and appeared in January 1969, but nobody has claimed responsibility for it.

The Cerne Giant is Dorset's most impressive hill-figure, best seen from the west of the main road, A352, near Cerne Abbas. Of many theories advanced about it the most logical is that it represents Hercules, whose cult had a revival during early Roman-British times in the second century A.D. This 180-feet high nude male figure, full of aggressive and sexual potency, is manifestly a focus of local legends associated with fertility in wives and livestock. The giant's very apparent phallus, ribs and nipples offended Victorian modesty, and these parts were allowed to become overgrown. When they were tidied up at the end of last century fears were expressed by churchmen that local morals would suffer.

The lowest lands of Wessex are today only a few feet above the level of the sea. For centuries their people have had to learn how to come to terms with water. Avalon and Sedgemoor must once have been places of island communities, as excavations of the Meare and Godney lake villages have proved. These flourished between 250 B.C. and A.D. 50, each a group of fifty or so huts built on manmade islands consisting of huge timbers supported on piles driven into the mud at the bottom of pools, and reached from the shore by a wooden causeway and drawbridge. The villagers were fishermen, farmers and hunters, who cultivated mainland fields and grazed livestock, and it is thought that the communities ended after finally being flooded out. We know more about these lake-dwellers than we do about Glastonbury, which is not mentioned until 658, when Saxons had settled there, but its name has an older Celtic connotation.

Glastonbury Tor is the commanding landmark of the Isle of Avalon. From the Mendips and Poldens, from the rounded hills to the east of the Foss Way, its conical profile constantly attracts the eye, just as the mind is drawn to its associations and legends. England's first Christian altar hallowed the earliest monastery at Glastonbury. Its stones today speak poetry, piety and praise, as well as the vandalism of Tudor times. Aldhelm knew Glastonbury, but Dunstan was its greatest abbot, under whom the monastery prospered, a combination of university, missionary centre, commercial and industrial enterprise and landowner.

Its monks had vineyards at Glastonbury, Wedmore, Meare and Pilton, where vines were grown on the sunny southern slopes of the hill in 1189. The present owners of Pilton Manor, Mr and Mrs Nigel de Marsac Godden, reintroduced vines in 1966 and 1968, the vineyards now extending to about 15 acres. When Christie's held a tasting in September 1976, of six English wines and six comparable European ones, a Riesling–Silvaner white wine from Pilton Manor vineyards was judged the best. The vineyard is open daily for the sale of wines and vines, and on Sundays during late summer you can wander round the vineyard and estate and sample the wines.

Between the tenth and fourteenth centuries the swamps, marshes

Above: *Glastonbury Abbey, where King Arthur and Queen Guinevere are said to have been buried.*

Opposite: *Glastonbury Tor (the Isle of Avalon of the Arthurian legends), Somerset, seen from the south.*

Withies drying at East Lyng, Sedgemoor, Somerset.

and lagoons of the Somerset levels were drained by the abbeys of Glastonbury, Muchelney and Athelney, producing the pattern of rhines we see today. Between these osier-fringed ditches, which for centuries have also served as irrigation channels and means of communication, broad, rich pastures have emerged, fine grazing-lands, and, on the slightly higher land, orchards. Roads across Avalon and Sedgemoor today take the form of raised causeways, and the willows which border them act as visible lifelines on occasions when the waters rise. Between the trees is the causeway, beyond them the rhines.

The low range of Polden Hills separates Avalon from Sedgemoor, the land of Arthur from the land of Alfred, apple-orchards from peat and basket country. Osier-willows are commonest in Sedgemoor, green or purple stemmed. After being cut back, plants grow a cluster of shoots, reaching six feet in a good summer, harvested each year to obtain good plant lengths, stripped of their bark to give white willow or boiled with it on to yield buff-coloured willow. Fishermen's crab and lobster pots, agricultural baskets, rustic furniture, all originate from the osiers of Sedgemoor.

The view towards Dundon Hills and Somerton Uplands from Walton Hill on the Polden Ridge. Evening sunlight throws long shadows across the levels of Butleigh Moor and Somerton Moor.

Peat of lowland country is far less acid than its upland counterpart, and is therefore much more useful horticulturally. Mechanization has transformed the industry in the Somerset lowlands, where peat has accumulated over 6,000 years and is now being exploited to the extent of over 60,000 tons a year. Even at this rate deposits are calculated to last for another fifty years. After being dug and cut, it stands for a short while in low piles, then the blocks are built up into tall conical ruckles to dry out thoroughly before finally being shredded.

The road from Glastonbury to Taunton crosses King's Sedgemoor and passes Burrow Mump, a smaller version of the Tor, and also crowned with a chapel dedicated to St Michael. Almost certainly this hill would have been a forward observation post for Alfred, during the period from January to Easter 878, when he hid from the Danes on the two-acre islet of Athelney at the junction of the Rivers Parret and Tone. Since during that time he frequently harried the enemy they could not have been far away, probably on the Polden ridge. On Athelney, following his victory over the Danes, Alfred founded an abbey as an act of thanksgiving, but it failed to flourish after Saxon times and nothing remains of it above ground. There is, however, near a group of farm buildings, a Georgian monument which is a somewhat tatty reminder of Athelney's association with Alfred, an insignificant place for the virtual rebirth of the English kingdom.

To the north is Weston Zoyland, whose parish register records the beginnings of the last battle fought on English soil, on 6 July 1685; between royalist troops and the Duke of Monmouth's forces. The Battle of Sedgemoor lasted an hour and a half, and the details are statistically cold.

> There was killed upon the spott of the King's souldiers sixteen; ffive of them buried in the church, the rest in the churchyard, and they had all of them Christian buriall. One hundred or more of the King's souldiers wounded; of which wounds many died, of which wee have no certaine account. There was killed of the rebels upon the spott about 300; hanged with us 22, of which 4 were hanged in chains. About 500 prisoners brought into our church, of which there was 79 wounded, and 5 of them died of their wounds in our church.

Shortly afterwards 22 were executed outside the church, the remaining prisoners lodged in various West Country jails pending the next assizes. Bussex Rhine, over which Monmouth's men could not find their way, and which thus confined them as sitting ducks for the royalists, has been filled in, and the land where royalists were camped now has orchards, houses and gardens. Weston Zoyland church has changed but little, its slender tower a better memorial to the unhappy affair than the meagre stone by the Taunton road.

When large areas of the English landscape were planned, remodelled and enclosed between 1700 and 1830, woods, forests and heaths were left on one side basically untouched. In Wessex the gravelly landscape of the Hampshire–Surrey border, the New Forest area and the heathlands of east Dorset remained little altered, at least until military authorities and government departments got their hands on them. Of the ancient woodlands only fragments survive, and these are more and more emaciated. If during medieval times you had stood on any high ground in Wessex your view would have shown a much more wooded countryside than appears today. Clay vales of Dorset and Wiltshire would have resembled oceans of tree-tops, mainly oak and ash, elm, lime and maple. The downs themselves had miles and miles of beechwoods, and where forests thinned out, and on heaths, silver birches predominated.

Large areas of Wessex were 'forest' in the technical sense, particularly during the two centuries following the Conquest. It was country set aside as royal game preserves, the successor to Saxon hunting parks, in which Norman kings introduced the forest laws, which reached their peak during the latter part of the twelfth century.

To the east of Alton the forests of Alice Holt and Woolmer, almost adjoining each other, are remnants of the great belt of woodland which once extended from the Thames at Windsor, through Berkshire and Hampshire to the south coast. Pines replace deciduous trees and the deer have gone. In Gilbert White's day Woolmer was a treeless heathland dominated by bracken, a "hungry, sandy, barren waste". Over a century later W. H.

Hudson could describe it as "all covered by the shaggy mantle of the trees . . . where the ling forms a thick undergrowth".

On the edge of the downs in the Selborne area woodland cover takes the form of hangers. White made his Selborne Hanger famous, but all of these hanging beechwoods have their appeal, green-leaved backcloths to views from the vales, and from their crests the sort of scene which surprised and delighted Cobbett when he first encountered Hawkley Hanger: "It was like looking from the top of a castle down into the sea, except that the valley was land and not water . . . These hangers are woods on the sides of very steep hills. The trees and underwood hang, in some sort, to the ground, instead of standing on it." The description is equally applicable today, and the Hampshire hangers are one of its greatest delights.

But it is the New Forest which is Hampshire's and England's best-known and best-loved forest. The 'New' came in the eleventh century to this huge area of undulating country with fine woods of oak and beech, separated by large areas of sandy heathland. By the fifth and sixth centuries it was mainly common grazing land, but some time in the tenth century it became a royal hunting forest. This did not necessarily involve wholesale appropriation of private property, but did impose a special code of restrictive laws. William I enlarged the old Saxon forest in 1079 without the destruction of churches, villages and farms which has been attributed to him. Since so much of the area had poor sandy soil it could never have supported much population. As it is, the existing peasant farming economy, dependent on rights of common pasturage in particular, kept these rights. Saxon and Norman kings were very careful to ensure this, proof that such rights antedated the formation of royal forests. The right to hunt deer in a royal forest was exercised by the Norman kings, fatally so in the case of William II. Forest laws protected the deer's needs, food, coverts for breeding, and open spaces in which to roam freely. Tenement holders in the forest were allowed to make enclosures by erecting fences *not* to keep deer out, but to keep their own stock *in*. Commoners did have the right to graze cattle in the forest for a month in the summer and five in winter, probably to help keep down undergrowth. Pigs were allowed two months' grazing for pannage (acorns and other tree-seeds), but breeding sows may now graze throughout the year.

In the seventeenth century the New Forest became a source of timber for building ships of the English fleet. A House of Commons Journal records that in 1608 there were 123,927 sound trees in the forest, but a century later this had fallen to 12,476. Forest management was not then understood, although both Charles II and William III did some new planting. For a time the New Forest had its own shipbuilding yard, Buckler's Hard, founded about 1724 by John, second Duke of Montagu, mainly as a port for trading with his West Indian estates on St Lucia and St Vincent. When the commercial project fell through, Buckler's Hard concentrated on ship-

Buckler's Hard: an eighteenth-century village where ship-building was an important industry. The chapel is at the first door on the left, the master builder's house at the far end.

building, and between 1745 and 1822 57 naval vessels and 15 merchant ships were constructed there. Gilpin, at the end of the eighteenth century, was not impressed: "The large timber yards, houses, and ships on the stocks make a violent chasm in the landscape". Now it is all very peaceful, with wistful memories of the past encapsulated in the Maritime Museum. Indeed, Buckler's Hard is itself a museum piece, where conservation and commercialism are mutually dependent. The two-mile walk by the Beaulieu River up to Beaulieu gives us easily the best approach to this attractive village, now better known for the Motor Museum than the Cistercian abbey adjoining it, which was founded by King John and destroyed by Henry VIII, when it came into the hands of the Montagu family, who rebuilt the gatehouse in 1872 and now live there.

In 1851 the Deer Removal Act saw the start of disafforestation of the New Forest, and in 1877 the ancient Court of Verderers was reconstituted, to safeguard the interests of commoners, limit the Crown's power of enclosure, and to make statutory provision for forest amenities. In 1919 the Forestry Commission was established, taking over control of the New Forest five years later, and working to an increasing degree with the Verderers' Court. Of its 144 square miles, about 103 are under public ownership, Crown land available for access and public recreation, as well as being a huge reserve of timber, grazing land for thousands of ponies and cattle, and a vast reservoir of wild life. Since 1964 ornamental tree-planting has been allowed, together with the establishment of a number of well-equipped and very popular camping and caravan sites.

Savernake Forest in Wiltshire was a royal forest for several hundred years, and subsequently passed through the Seymours to the Earl of Ailesbury in 1696, and is still owned by the Ailesbury family, although 2,000 acres are leased to the Forestry Commission. The thick woodlands of Savernake, planted by succeeding generations, give it a parkland ornamentation, with few open

Savernake Forest, Wiltshire: the Grand Avenue, passing through the plantation of beech trees, is four miles long.

glades, no barren patches, but the Georgian formality of splendid beech avenues several undulating miles in length.

Wiltshire's other forests mainly survive in name, Braden Forest in the north, which was disafforested by Charles II, with Melksham and Pewsham Forests extending south from it, almost linking up with Clarendon Forest east of Salisbury. Clarendon Palace was for four centuries one of the favourite homes of kings, many of whom gradually added to the Norman structure until in size it was second only to the Palace of Westminster, spread over eighteen acres and unfortified. After the Wars of the Roses it was no longer used, and slowly deteriorated into oblivion, rather like the great forest which surrounded it.

Selwood Forest originally covered about 200 square miles of countryside along the Wiltshire–Somerset border, from the Avon in the north to the Dorset border in the south. In Saxon times Aldhelm made missionary journeys along its margins, and it became a royal forest in the twelfth century. Yet by 1350 it had diminished to a tenth of its former size, and by 1540 it was merely a series of scattered woodlands from Bradford-on-Avon to Shaftesbury. In the late eighteenth century Billingsley wrote that 18,000 of its 20,000 acres had been converted into pasture and arable, the rest being coppice of oak and ash, very much as it looks today, although there are many fine shelter-belts of beech, seen especially well from the road which runs almost through the heart of old Selwood, between Frome, Maiden Bradley and Mere. Villages are widely dispersed, and although good stone was available from quarries at Chilmark and Doulting, architecturally Selwood has nothing outstanding, other than the great mansions at Longleat and Stourhead. Yet there is what I can only call a 'Wessex quality' about its landscape, possibly arising from its Aldhelm and Alfred associations.

Wiltshire shares Selwood with Somerset, and Cranborne Chase with Dorset, although only a small area of this old royal forest is still within Wiltshire. From 980 till 1102 Cranborne was the seat of the Chase Court as well as of a small Benedictine monastery, both of which gave it some standing. The Cecils had rebuilt Cranborne House at the beginning of the seventeenth century, around a thirteenth-century hunting lodge used occasionally by King John and his successors who hunted deer in the 300 square miles of land extending from Shaftesbury to Salisbury.

In the 1880s General Pitt-Rivers lived near Cranborne and carried out wide-scale archaeological excavations in the area which revealed evidence proving that it had been far more densely inhabited in Roman and pre-Roman times than it had been since.

King John's hunting lodge at Tollard Royal, Wiltshire.

Showing more interest in creating ornamental pleasure-gardens with pavilions and a bandstand than in hunting the 10,000 deer in the Chase, Pitt-Rivers' activities brought a new, if temporary, fame to the ancient forest. More recently, under the pioneering influence of Mr Rolf Gardiner of the Springhead Estates near Fontmell Magna, the Cranborne Chase Co-operative Forestry Group has brought new life to the district, using the idea of large-scale planning and management co-operation, so that farming and afforestation are not carried out on a piecemeal basis. Local crafts and

Part of a hurdle made near Sixpenny Handley, Cranborne Chase.

industries are encouraged, such as wood-turning and wattle hurdle-making, using hazel underwoods which grow profusely, especially around Sixpenny Handley. Cranborne Chase has the biggest acreage of open woodland with coppice in Wessex, mainly oak and hazel, but as in other areas new plantations are of conifers rather than hardwoods.

Cranborne can be thought of as being at the northern tip of the Dorset heaths, which curve down to Studland and westwards to Dorchester, the other apexes. 'Egdon Heath' was the term with which Hardy lumped together all the scattered heaths along the southern edge of this large triangle, and although much of it has changed, especially over the past sixty years, seen at detail-extinguishing dusk the mystic brooding character of the great heath returns. Heather, bracken and rhododendron groves cover some of its unforested western parts, but most of its wild life and its wilderness quality remain. Perhaps the strongest impressions of the heath are to be sensed and seen in the rough rectangle bounded by Wareham, Wool, Bere Regis and Lytchett Minster, part of it being a Nature Reserve and part afforested (with conifers), but there are good stretches of heather, furze, shady tracks and quiet pools. Similarly, between Wareham and the Purbeck Hills heathland predominates, one of England's oldest and least man-handled landscapes. Even though the Winfrith Heath Atomic Energy Station is not far away — and needed a special Act of Parliament to eliminate ancient common rights on it — I feel that here on these Dorset heaths is an immutable, primitive, distinctive view of Wessex. Let the final words appropriately come from Hardy who described the scenery of Egdon as "Majestic in its admonitions, grand in its simplicity . . . The great inviolate place had an ancient permanence which the sea cannot claim . . . The sea changed, the rivers, the villages, and the people changed, yet Egdon remained."

INDEX

Numbers in bold indicate illustrations

M